English for international communication

Jack C. Richards
Chuck Sandy

Teacher's Manual

CAMBRIDGE
UNIVERSITY PRESS

Published by the Press Syndicate of the University of Cambridge
The Pitt Building, Trumpington Street, Cambridge CB2 1RP
40 West 20th Street, New York, NY 10011-4211, USA
10 Stamford Road, Oakleigh, Melbourne, Australia

First published 1995
Second printing 1995

Printed in the United States of America

ISBN 0 521 46742 X   Intro Teacher's Manual
ISBN 0 521 46744 6   Intro Student's Book
ISBN 0 521 46743 8   Intro Workbook
ISBN 0 521 46741 1   Intro Class Cassettes

Split editions:
ISBN 0 521 47185 0   Intro Student's Book A
ISBN 0 521 47186 9   Intro Student's Book B
ISBN 0 521 47187 7   Intro Workbook A
ISBN 0 521 47188 5   Intro Workbook B
ISBN 0 521 46740 3   Intro Student Cassette A
ISBN 0 521 47189 3   Intro Student Cassette B

Book design: Circa 86, Inc.
Layout and design services: Adventure House
Cover design: Tom Wharton

Illustrators:
Adventure House, 98
Ken Call, 141, 146
Gene Mater, 142, 144
Wally Neibart, 147, 153

Contents

Plan of Intro Student's Book

	Topics	Functions	Grammar
UNIT 1	**Topics** Alphabet; greetings and leave-takings; titles of address; classroom objects; telephone numbers	**Functions** Introducing yourself; spelling names and words; saying phone numbers; giving classroom instructions	**Grammar** Possessive adjectives *my, your, his,* and *her;* the verb *be:* affirmative statements and contractions; numbers 1–10; articles *a* and *an;* imperatives (affirmative)
UNIT 2	**Topics** Personal items, possessions, and locations in a room	**Functions** Naming objects; finding the owner of an item; asking for and giving location	**Grammar** Plurals; *this* and *these;* possessive of names; possessive adjectives; the verb *be:* yes/no questions and short answers with *it* and *they;* prepositions of place
UNIT 3	**Topics** Countries; regions; nationalities; languages	**Functions** Asking for and giving information about country of origin, nationality, native language, and geographical locations	**Grammar** Affirmative and negative statements with *be;* adjectives of nationality; questions and short answers with *be*
UNIT 4	**Topics** Clothing, colors; weather, temperatures, and seasons of the year	**Functions** Asking about and describing clothing; talking about current activities; talking about the weather	**Grammar** Present continuous: affirmative and negative statements; numbers to 100; adjectives after *be*

Review of Units 1–4

	Topics	Functions	Grammar
UNIT 5	**Topics** Times of the day, clock time; daily activities; Saturday chores	**Functions** Asking for and telling time; asking about and describing current activities	**Grammar** Present continuous: *what + doing,* yes/no questions and short answers; Wh-questions; adverbs of time
UNIT 6	**Topics** Transportation; family relationships; daily habits; days of the week	**Functions** Asking for and giving information about where you live, how you go to work, and what you do every day	**Grammar** Present tense: affirmative and negative statements; third-person singular endings; irregular verbs and yes/no and Wh-questions; present time expressions
UNIT 7	**Topics** Homes; rooms; furniture	**Functions** Asking about and describing different homes; saying what furniture is in a room	**Grammar** Present tense: yes/no questions and short answers; *There's /There are* and *There's no/There aren't any*
UNIT 8	**Topics** Occupations; places of work; salaries	**Functions** Asking and giving information about what people do, where they work, and how they like their jobs	**Grammar** Present tense: Wh-questions with *do;* descriptive adjectives; placement of adjectives before nouns

Review of Units 5–8

Spelling Differences Between American and British English

Words in the *Intro* Student's Book that have a different spelling in British English:

American spelling	British spelling
center	centre
color	colour
favorite	favourite
gray	grey
driver's license	driving license
neighbor	neighbour
practice (verb)	practise (verb)
yogurt	yoghourt/yoghurt

Phonetic Symbols

iy	(sheep)	ʊ	(book)	k	(key)	w	(window)
ɪ	(ship)	uw	(boot)	g	(girl)	y	(yellow)
ɛ	(yes)	ay	(fine)	s	(sun)	h	(how)
ey	(train)	ɔy	(boy)	z	(zoo)	θ	(think)
æ	(hat)	aw	(house)	ʃ	(shoe)	ð	(the feather)
ʌ	(cup)	ɜr	(word)	ʒ	(television)	m	(mouth)
ə	(a banana)	p	(pen)	tʃ	(chair)	n	(nose)
ər	(letter)	b	(baby)	dʒ	(joke)	ŋ	(ring)
ɑ	(father)	t	(tie)	f	(fan)	l	(letter)
ɔ	(ball)	d	(door)	v	(van)	r	(rain)
ow	(no)						

Introduction

Interchange is a multi-level course in English as a second or foreign language for young adults and adults. The course covers the skills of listening, speaking, reading, and writing, with particular emphasis on listening and speaking. The primary goal of the course is to teach communicative competence – that is, the ability to communicate in English according to the situation, purpose, and role of the participants. *Interchange* reflects the fact that English is the world's major language of international communication and is not limited to any one country, region, or culture. The *Intro* level is designed for beginning students needing a thorough presentation of basic functions, grammar, and vocabulary. It prepares students to enter Level 1 of the course.

COURSE LENGTH

Interchange is a self-contained course covering all four language skills. Each level provides between 60 and 90 hours of class instruction. Depending on how the book is used, however, more or less time may be utilized. The Teacher's Manual gives detailed suggestions for optional and extra practice activities to extend each unit. Where less time is available, a level can be taught in approximately 60 hours by reducing the amount of time spent on Interchange Activities; reading, writing, optional and extra practice activities; and the Workbook.

COURSE COMPONENTS OF *INTRO*

Student's Book The Student's Book contains sixteen units, with a review unit after every four units. There are four review units in all. Following Unit 16 is a set of communicative activities called Interchange Activities, one for each unit of the book. Word lists at the end of the Student's Book contain key vocabulary and expressions used in each unit. The Student's Book is available in split editions, A and B, each containing eight units and providing from 30 to 45 hours of class instruction.

Teacher's Manual A separate Teacher's Manual contains detailed suggestions on how to teach the course, lesson-by-lesson notes, an extensive set of follow-up activities, complete answer keys to the Student's Book and Workbook exercises, four tests for use in class, test answer keys, and transcripts of those listening activities not printed in the Student's Book or in the tests. The tests can be photocopied and distributed to students after each review unit is completed.

Workbook The Workbook contains stimulating and varied exercises that provide additional practice on the teaching points presented in the Student's Book. A variety of exercise types is used to develop students' skills in grammar, reading, writing, spelling, vocabulary, and pronunciation. The Workbook can be used both for classwork and for homework. The Workbook is available in split editions.

Class Cassettes A set of three cassettes for class use accompanies the Student's Book. The cassettes contain recordings of the word power activities, conversations, grammar focus summaries, pronunciation exercises, listening activities, and readings, as well as recordings of the listening exercises used in the tests. A variety of native-speaker voices and accents is used, along with some non-native speakers of English. Exercises that are recorded on the cassettes are indicated with the symbol 🔘 .

Student Cassettes Two cassettes are available for students to use for self-study. The Student Cassettes contain recordings of conversations, readings, grammar presentations, pronunciation practice, and some vocabulary exercises from the Student's Book. Student Cassette A corresponds to Units 1–8 and Student Cassette B to Units 9–16.

APPROACH AND METHODOLOGY

Interchange teaches students to use English for everyday situations and purposes related to work, school, social life, and leisure. The underlying philosophy of the course is that learning a second language is more rewarding, meaningful, and effective when the language is used for authentic communication. Information-sharing activities provide a maximum amount of student-generated communication. Throughout *Interchange,* students have the opportunity to personalize the language they learn and make use of their own life experiences and world knowledge.

   Interchange is based on the following methodological principles.

Integration of form and function

In *Interchange,* grammar is seen as an important component of communicative competence. However, grammar is always presented communicatively, with exercises focusing on both accuracy and fluency. In this way, there is a link between grammatical form and communicative function. Fluency is achieved through information gap tasks, pair work, group work, and role plays.

Emphasis on meaningful communicative practice

Throughout the course, students have the opportunity to personalize the language they learn, to make use of their own world knowledge, and to express their ideas and opinions. Information-sharing activities allow for a maximum amount of student-generated communication.

Focus on productive and receptive skills

In *Interchange,* both production and comprehension form the basis of language learning. Students' productive skills are developed through speaking and writing tasks, and their receptive skills are developed through listening and reading. The course teaches students to understand language that is at a higher level than they can produce, and this prepares them to make the transition from the classroom to the real world.

Variety of learning modes

Different kinds of learning activities are used throughout the course. These include whole class activities and tasks done in small groups, pairs, or individually. This variation allows for a change of pace within lessons. The extensive use of pair work and group work activities in *Interchange* makes the course ideal in both large and small classes and gives students a greater amount of individual practice and interaction with others in the classroom.

Teacher's and learners' roles

The teacher's role in *Interchange* is to present and model new learning items; however, during pair work, group work, and role play activities, the teacher's role is that of a facilitator. Here the teacher's primary function is to prepare students for an activity and then let them complete it using their own resources. During this phase, the teacher gives informal feedback and encourages maximum participation.

   The learners' role in *Interchange* is to participate actively and creatively in learning, using both the materials they study in the course and their own knowledge and language resources. Students are treated as intelligent adults with ideas and opinions of their own. Students learn through interacting with others in pair or group activities and draw on both previous learning as well as their own communicative skills.

Teacher-friendly and student-friendly presentation

Interchange is easy to follow, with clearly identified teaching points, carefully organized and sequenced units, comfortable pacing, and a variety of stimulating and enjoyable tasks.

SYLLABUS

Interchange has an integrated, multi-skills syllabus that links grammar, communicative functions, and topics (see Plan of *Intro* Level on pages iv–vii). The syllabus also contains the four skills of listening, speaking, reading, and writing, as well as pronunciation and vocabulary. It is carefully graded, with a gradual progression of teaching items and frequent reviews.

Grammar   The course has a graded grammar syllabus. The *Intro* level contains the essential grammar, tenses, and structures needed for a basic level of language proficiency. The grammar points are introduced in communicative contexts, with accuracy-based activities leading to fluency-based communicative practice.

Functions   A functional syllabus parallels the grammar syllabus in the course. Each unit presents several key functions (e.g., making introductions, asking the time, asking for personal information) that are linked to the grammar points and topics of the unit. The *Intro* level presents about 35 essential functions, which enable students to participate in basic communication on a wide variety of topics.

Topics   The course deals with contemporary and adult topics that are of interest to learners of different cultural backgrounds. Information is presented that can serve as a basis for cross-cultural comparison and that both students and teachers will find stimulating and enjoyable. The topics have been selected for their interest to both homogeneous and heterogeneous classes.

Listening   The course reflects current understanding of the nature of listening comprehension in second and foreign language learning. Two kinds of listening skills are taught. *Top-down processing skills* require students to use background knowledge, the situation, context, and topic to arrive at comprehension through using key words and predicting; *bottom-up processing skills* require students to decode individual words in the message to derive meaning. Both of these skills are used in listening for gist, listening for details, and inferring meaning from context. The recordings on the Class Cassettes contain conversations with the natural pauses, hesitations, and interruptions that occur in real speech.

Speaking Skills   Speaking skills are a central focus of *Interchange* and of the *Intro* level. Many elements in the syllabus (e.g., grammar, functions, topics, listening, pronunciation, vocabulary) provide support for oral communication. Speaking activities in the course focus on conversational fluency, such as the ability to open and close conversations, introduce and develop conversational topics, take turns in conversations, use communication strategies and clarification requests, and understand and use idiomatic expressions. In addition, a range of useful conversational expressions is taught.

Reading   The course treats reading as an important way of developing receptive language and vocabulary. At the same time, the reading passages provide stimulating adult content that both students and teachers will enjoy. The *Intro* readings, which begin in Unit 5, are generally personal accounts of people's everyday lives. Also included are advertisements, articles, and extracts from travel guides. The accompanying activities develop the reading skills of guessing words from context, reading for main ideas, skimming, scanning, and making inferences, as well as reading for pleasure and for information. This approach also develops both top-down and bottom-up processing skills in reading.

Writing   Writing activities in *Interchange* focus on different forms of writing (e.g., descriptions, instructions, narratives). The *Intro* writing activities generally ask students to compose five or more sentences on a topic of personal interest. Writing is often used as a basis for other activities, such as grammar practices, games, and information-sharing activities.

Pronunciation   The *Intro* level treats pronunciation as an integral part of grammar, and of oral proficiency in general. The pronunciation exercises focus on important features of spoken English, including stress, intonation, reductions, and sound contrasts.

Vocabulary   Vocabulary plays a key role in *Interchange. Intro* teaches a productive vocabulary of about 1000 words (about 600 in *Intro* A, and 400 in *Intro* B). Productive vocabulary is presented through a wide variety of vocabulary exercises and through speaking and grammar activities. Receptive vocabulary is introduced through reading and listening exercises. Vocabulary learning is often enhanced through the presentation of words in semantically related sets or categories.

UNIT STRUCTURE AND ORGANIZATION

Although the sequencing of exercise types varies throughout *Interchange,* a typical unit presents two main topics or functions, each with a cycle of related exercises. The exercise types listed in the table below are used throughout the course.

Exercise Title	*Purpose*
Snapshot	These exercises contain interesting, real-world information that introduces the topic of a unit or cycle. They also build receptive vocabulary. The information in the Snapshot is presented in a graphic form, which makes it easy to read.
Word Power	These vocabulary exercises present key words related to the topic of the unit that can be used throughout the unit.
Conversation	Conversation exercises introduce new grammar points and functions. They present the grammar in a situational context and also serve as models for speaking tasks.
Grammar Focus	These exercises present summaries of new grammar items followed by controlled and freer communicative practice of the grammar.
Pair Work Group Work Role Play	These oral exercises provide freer and more personalized practice of the new teaching points and increase the opportunity for individual student practice.
Pronunciation	These exercises focus on pronunciation features occurring in the Conversation and Grammar Focus exercises.
Listening	These exercises provide listening practice related to the topic of the unit and develop students' receptive skills.
Reading	Reading exercises develop reading skills as well as receptive language and vocabulary. Most include a writing task as well.
Interchange Activities	These activities provide a communicative extension to the unit. They allow students to use the language and skills in the unit creatively. These activities are a key part of each unit.

REVIEW UNITS, KEY VOCABULARY, AND TESTS

Review Units Review units occur after every four units in the *Intro* level; they contain exercises that review the teaching points from the four preceding units. They are mainly speaking and listening exercises that review grammar, vocabulary, and conversational expressions, and practice listening. They can also be used as informal tests of students' oral production and listening.

Key Vocabulary These lists at the end of the Student's Book contain not only the key productive vocabulary used in each unit, but conversational expressions and receptive vocabulary as well. The vocabulary is listed in grammatical categories (nouns, verbs, prepositions, adjectives, etc.), and offers a convenient review and summary.

Tests There are four tests, one for use after every four units of the Student's Book. The tests enable the teacher to evaluate students' progress in the course and to decide if any areas of the course need further review. The tests are on pages 140–157 of this Teacher's Manual and may be photocopied for class use. Complete information on administering and scoring the tests is located at the back of the Teacher's Manual, along with the answer keys.

GENERAL GUIDELINES FOR TEACHING *INTERCHANGE*

The philosophy underlying *Interchange* is that learning a second or foreign language is more meaningful and effective when the language is used for real communication instead of being studied as an end in itself. *Interchange* follows a multi-skills syllabus in which each component of the course is linked. For example, a vocabulary-building exercise can serve as the basis for a speaking task, a role play activity may lead into a listening task, or a grammar exercise may often prepare students for a functional activity.

The following general guidelines can be used when teaching the *Intro* level of the course.

Teaching vocabulary

Vocabulary is a key element in *Interchange* because a wide productive vocabulary is essential in learning a second or foreign language. Before presenting any exercise, it is helpful to see which words are needed in order to complete the task and which are not essential – not all new vocabulary needs presentation in advance. Students should recognize that in most language-learning situations they will encounter vocabulary they do not know; however, they do not need to understand every word. In addition, students need to understand that when they encounter an unknown word, they can often guess its meaning from the situation or context.

Where it is necessary to pre-teach new vocabulary, use the following strategies:

■ Ask students to look at the context in which a word is used and to try to find any clues to its meaning. Encourage students to guess meanings of new words.

■ Where necessary, provide the meanings of words through photos and illustrations, mime, synonyms, examples, or translations. It is not necessary to give long explanations.

■ In general, discourage the use of dictionaries during class time, except where it is suggested within an exercise.

■ After teaching a unit, ask students to review the Key Vocabulary at the back of their book to see how many of the words they can remember.

■ Encourage students to keep a vocabulary notebook and to write down new words as they learn them.

Teaching grammar

Correct use of grammar is an essential aspect of communicative competence. In *Interchange,* grammatical accuracy is an integral part of proficiency, but it is always a means to an end rather than an end in itself. It is important to remember that second language learners do not develop grammatical proficiency by studying rules. They acquire new grammar by using the language in situations where it is needed. This means that grammar should always be practiced communicatively. However, language learning also involves testing out hypotheses about how the language works. In developing these hypotheses, some students will rely more on grammatical explanations than others.

   In the Grammar Focus exercises, the information in the color panels should be used to explain new grammar points. Give additional examples and explanations if necessary to clarify the grammar, but avoid turning any lesson into a grammar class. Lead students into the practice activities for the new grammar points as quickly as possible. Then use the students' performance on these activities to decide if further clarification or grammar work is needed. There are many additional grammar exercises in the Workbook that can be used as a follow-up.

Teaching listening skills

The Listening exercises are designed to bridge the gap between the classroom and the real world. While most of the Listening exercises have the heading "Listening," there are also some that act as an extension of the Conversations.

   When teaching listening, it is important to remind students that in most listening situations the aim is *not* to remember the specific words or phrases used but to extract the main ideas or information. To help students do this, the Listening exercises usually contain a task that helps students identify a purpose for listening, which encourages them to ignore language that is not related to this purpose. When presenting an exercise, it is also important to prepare students for the task through pre-listening activities. These include asking questions about the topic, asking students to make predictions, and making use of the context provided by the pictures and the situation.

Teaching speaking skills

A number of different kinds of activities focus on speaking skills: Conversations, Pair Work, Group Work, Class Activities, and Interchange Activities. Each of these activities involves different learning arrangements in the class.

Conversations   These exercises can be used for both listening and speaking practice. They usually require students to work with one or two partners. Since the Conversation exercises model conversational expressions and pronunciation and present new teaching items, accurate repetition of the Conversations on the tape is important. However, students should not be asked to memorize them. When students practice Conversations, teach them to use the "Look Up and Say" technique. For this technique, students look at the page and then look up and say their line while maintaining eye contact with their partner. This encourages students to avoid a "reading" pronunciation and intonation when practicing Conversation exercises together.

Pair Work   The course makes extensive use of pair work activities. These give students a chance for individual practice and maximize the amount of speaking practice they get in each class. Some students may be unfamiliar with pair work tasks and may not think that they can learn from their classmates. If so, remind students that practicing with a partner is a useful way of improving their fluency in English and gives them more opportunity to speak English in class.

Group Work and Class Activities   The course also makes frequent use of group work and whole class activities. In the group work activities, students usually work in groups of three to five. Sometimes one student is the group secretary and takes notes to report back to the class later. In the class activities, the whole class is involved (e.g., completing a survey or gathering information).

Interchange Activities   These exercises are important for developing fluency and are also fun. They focus on the creative use of language and require students to draw on their own language resources to complete a task or to improvise and keep a conversation going.

In doing these types of speaking activities, the following guidelines are important:

■ Make sure students fully understand the task and have the information they need. Assign roles and model the task where necessary.

■ Set up pairs or groups so that students of different ability levels and different first languages can work together. This arrangement will encourage students to help and learn from each other.

■ Vary the pair or group arrangements so that students do not always work with the same classmates.

■ Discourage use of the students' native languages when doing an activity, and get them to use as much English as possible in class.

Giving Feedback   It is important to give clear feedback on students' performance, but feedback should not inhibit students' attempts to communicate. Accuracy in speaking a new language takes a long time to accomplish in second language learning, and both student and teacher need to realize this. Some aspects of language will be more difficult than others, depending on the students' levels of proficiency or native tongues. Immediate results are not always apparent. The teacher will need to assess which aspects of the students' performance are worth drawing attention to at any particular time in their language development.

It is better to give occasional but focused feedback on one thing at a time than to overwhelm a student with too much information. The teacher will have many opportunities to give individual feedback when students are working in pairs or groups. During these activities, the teacher can move around the class giving feedback on grammar, pronunciation, and vocabulary when needed. This is also an opportunity to determine if additional practice work is needed. Students often prefer this type of private or personalized feedback to feedback given in front of the whole class.

Teaching reading skills

The approach to the teaching of reading in *Interchange* is similar to that used for teaching listening. The purpose for reading determines the strategy the students should use, such as reading the passage for main ideas (i.e., skimming), looking quickly for specific information in the passage (i.e., scanning), reading more slowly for detailed understanding, reading for the author's attitude, or reading to identify a sequence of events. It is important not to present each reading exercise as if it always requires the same approach (e.g., 100 percent comprehension of the passage). When students are doing a reading exercise, check that they are using appropriate reading strategies. For example:

■ Students should read silently and not subvocalize (i.e., pronounce words or move their lips while reading).

■ Students should read only with their eyes and not use a pencil or finger to follow the sentence they are reading.

■ Students should not use their dictionaries to look up every new word they encounter in a reading passage.

■ To encourage student interaction in the class, many comprehension tasks can be done as pair work. Sometimes reading activities can be assigned for homework if class time is short.

■ Choose the right moment to have students listen to the passage on tape. For some students this should be done right after the silent reading phase. Listening to the tape will aid comprehension by providing the proper phrasing and inflections. In most cases, however, it is best to play the tape after students have completed the comprehension activities. The added dimension of listening to the voices will motivate students to read the passage again.

Teaching writing skills

Writing activities in the *Intro* level are included within other exercises, such as Reading or Word Power. Students use the models in the book as a springboard for their own writing. It is good for students to become acquainted with these basic steps of the writing process:

Pre-writing phase: Through discussion of the topic, reading, or brainstorming, students generate ideas and collect vocabulary and information related to the topic, and then make notes.

Planning: Students use their ideas, information, vocabulary, and notes to plan their writing. They should quickly write a first draft without writing complete sentences. The focus here is on useful ideas, not on grammar and spelling.

Drafting: Students now write another draft with complete sentences.

Editing: Students check their writing for accuracy, concentrating on grammar, spelling, and punctuation.

TESTING STUDENTS' PROGRESS

The following testing procedures are suggested for use with *Interchange*.

Using the tests in the Teacher's Manual

Four tests are contained in the Teacher's Manual to assess students' learning (see pages 140–157). There is one test to be used after every four units. These are progress tests that assess students' learning of grammar, conversational expressions, vocabulary, and listening. (For testing students' oral performance, see the following section.) The tests draw on each set of four units as a whole and are not linked to specific exercises in each unit. Only items actively presented and practiced in the Student's Book are tested. Each test takes approximately 45 minutes to complete in class. A satisfactory rate of learning should lead to 80 percent and above accuracy. If students score lower than this, the teacher may wish to reteach some sections of the book, give additional supplementary exercises, or assign extra homework exercises. In addition to using these tests, the teacher can also informally check students' oral and written progress at the end of each unit.

Using tests prepared by the teacher

It is also possible to check students' progress at the end of each unit using teacher-prepared tests. When developing these tests, it is important to keep the following principles in mind:

■ The principal goal of *Interchange* is communicative competence. Test items should reflect use of language in communicative contexts rather than in isolation.

■ Test items should reflect the kind of practice activities used in a unit (i.e., test what has been taught and test it in a format similar to that in which it was presented in the unit).

- Distinguish between items that were presented receptively and those that were presented productively. Test productively only the language that students have practiced productively.

Here are some examples of possible test items:

1. Keeping a conversation going on a topic by asking follow-up questions.
2. Completing missing parts of a conversation, focusing on the grammar, vocabulary, or expressions in the unit.
3. Providing suitable conversational expressions for different purposes (e.g., greeting someone, giving the time).
4. Selecting an item from two or three choices, such as choosing an appropriate pronoun or adjective in a sentence.
5. Completing a sentence with the suitable form of a verb or the correct word.
6. Reordering scrambled sentences using the correct word order.
7. Choosing the correct lexical item to complete a sentence.
8. Supplying missing words in a passage, either by selecting from words given or using the cloze technique.
9. Completing a short writing task similar to one presented in the unit.
10. Answering questions or supplying information following a model provided in the unit.
11. Reading a sentence aloud with correct pronunciation.
12. Reading a passage similar to one in the unit and completing questions or a task based on it.

Other useful information on oral testing techniques can be found in *Testing Spoken Language* by Nic Underhill (Cambridge University Press, 1987).

HOW TO TEACH A TYPICAL UNIT IN *INTERCHANGE*

The unit-by-unit notes give detailed suggestions for teaching each unit. However, on a general basis, the following procedures can be used to teach *Interchange*.

Introduce the topic of the unit by asking questions and eliciting information from the students related to the theme or topic. Then explain what the students will study in the unit (i.e., mention the main topics, functions, and grammar as presented in the Plan of *Intro* Level on pp. iv–vii). Next present the exercises, using the following guidelines.

Snapshot

- Books closed. Introduce the topic by asking questions about it using language that is familiar to students. Use these questions to elicit or present the key vocabulary of the Snapshot and to ask for students' opinions on the topic they are going to read about.

- Books open. Lead the students through the information in the Snapshot. Go over any problems of comprehension as they arise.

- Students complete the task individually or in pairs.

- Students compare answers with a partner or around the class.

- As an alternative, ask students to read the Snapshot for homework and complete the task, using a dictionary. Then students can compare answers with a partner in class.

Word Power

- Introduce and model the pronunciation of the words in the exercise, or play the tape recording.

- Explain the task.

- Students complete the task individually or in pairs, without using a dictionary if possible.

- Students compare answers.

- Check students' answers.

Conversation

- Optional: Books open. Students cover the conversation. Use the picture to set the scene.

- Books closed. Before presenting the conversation, explain the situation. Write questions on the board based on the conversation for students to answer later.

- Play the conversation on the tape or read it aloud. Students listen for answers to the questions. Check students' answers.

- Books open. Play the tape again. Students listen only.

- Present the conversation line by line using the tape. Present new vocabulary, model pronunciation, and explain idiomatic expressions.

- Students practice the conversation in pairs. Use the Look Up and Say technique.

- After students have completed the subsequent activities in the cycle, you can come back to the conversation and have students adapt it by substituting their own information.

Grammar Focus

- Use the tape to present the sentences in the color panel.

- Give students additional examples to illustrate the grammar point where necessary. If appropriate, practice the sentences in the color panel as in a drill.

- Students complete the task. This can often be completed orally as a whole class activity before students complete it individually or in pairs. If necessary, students can write the answers on a separate piece of paper.

- Students compare answers in pairs.

- Call on students to read their answers aloud. Check and give feedback.

Pair Work

- Divide the class into pairs. If there is an odd number of students, form one set of three.

- Explain the task and model it with one or two students. Call on a pair of students to do the task as a further model if necessary.

- Set a time limit.

- Students practice in pairs. Move around the class and give help as needed.

- Optional: Students change partners and do the task again.

- Call on pairs of students to do the activity in front of the class.

Group Work

- Divide the class into groups of three to five.

- Explain the task and model it with some of the students.

- Set a time limit.

- Students practice in groups. Move around the class and give help as needed.

- Optional: Students form new groups and do the task again.

Pronunciation

- Use the tape to introduce the teaching point.

- Play the tape again. Students practice.

- Give additional examples for students to practice if necessary.

- Remind students of the pronunciation point when appropriate (i.e., during the Conversation and pair or group work tasks).

Listening

- Optional: Books open. Use the picture to set the scene.

- Books closed. Set the scene and explain the situation.

- Play the tape. Students listen for general comprehension. Point out any key vocabulary that is essential for the task. (The transcripts for all Listening recordings are printed in the Teacher's Manual after the exercise suggestions.)

- Books open. Explain the task. Remind students that they do not have to understand everything on the tape.

- Play the tape again once or twice. Students listen and complete the task.

- Students compare answers in pairs.

- Check students' answers.

Reading

- Before students read the passage, use questions to introduce the topic of the passage and to help establish background knowledge.

- Preview the vocabulary and pre-teach only key words that students might not be able to infer from context. Encourage students to guess the meanings of words using context clues.

- Explain the task.

- Students read the passage silently. Discourage students from using a pencil or finger to point at the text or from subvocalizing (i.e., pronouncing words silently) while reading.

- Students compare answers in pairs.

- Check students' answers.

- Optional: Play the tape as students read the passage again.

- Optional: Ask follow-up discussion questions.

Interchange Activities

These activities are found at the back of the Student's Book. There is one Interchange Activity for each unit in the book. Sometimes pairs of students will use different pages for role play or information gap tasks.

- Where necessary, assign the students roles (A, B, C, etc.) and their page numbers for the task.

- Model the activity. Encourage students to be creative. They should not refer back to the unit once they have begun the activity.

- Students do the task. Go around the class and give help as needed.

- Where appropriate, call on pairs of students to do the activity in front of the class.

Key Vocabulary

Students can use the Key Vocabulary as a review activity after each unit has been taught (e.g., for homework).

Workbook

Preview each unit of Workbook exercises before introducing the unit in class. Note that the Workbook exercises do not present teaching points in exactly the same sequence as the exercises in the Student's Book. Rather, the Workbook exercises are more integrative, often combining vocabulary and teaching points from two or more Student's Book exercises into one activity. The Workbook can be used in a number of ways:

- After students complete a Student's Book exercise, assign a Workbook exercise with the same teaching point.

- After completing a cycle in the Student's Book, assign the corresponding Workbook exercises. For most units, the first cycle in the Student's Book corresponds to the first two pages of the unit in the Workbook, and the second cycle to the second two pages.

- At the end of a unit, have students do all the Workbook exercises as a review.

- The Workbook exercises can be completed in class or as homework.

1 Hello. My name is Jennifer Wan.

This unit has two cycles and presents the language needed for names, introductions, greetings, and simple instructions in the classroom. It introduces the alphabet and the numbers zero through ten. It also focuses on questions and statements with the verb *be*.

UNIT PLAN

Cycle 1

1 Snapshot: *Introduces the topic of names in English*

2 Conversation: *Presents self-introductions and possessive pronouns*

3 The Alphabet: *Introduces the alphabet in English and practices spelling aloud*

4 Grammar Focus: *Practices the possessive adjectives* my, your, his, her

5 Listening: *Practices understanding names that are spelled aloud*

6 Conversation: *Introduces questions and statements with the verb* be

7 Grammar Focus: *Practices questions and statements with* be *and contractions*

WORKBOOK: Exercises 1–5 on pages 1 and 2

Cycle 2

8 Numbers: *Presents the numbers zero through ten*

Interchange 1: *An information-gap activity that reviews spelling names and understanding telephone numbers*

9 Listening: *Practices listening for telephone numbers*

10 Word Power: *Develops vocabulary for classroom objects; presents* a *and* an

11 Greetings and Titles: *Presents expressions for saying hello and good-bye*

12 Instructions: *Presents affirmative classroom commands*

WORKBOOK: Exercises 6–9 on pages 3 and 4

1 SNAPSHOT

SB p. 2 This activity introduces students to popular first names in the United States.

■ Books closed. To present the topic, write the words "name," "female," and "male" on the board in a chart like this:

NAME	
Female	Male

Show the meaning of "female" and "male" by pointing to students in the room. Show the meaning of "name" by taking attendance: Call out a student's name, and then write it on the board under "female" or "male." Stop when students understand the concepts.

■ Books open. Read the list of names aloud to the students as they follow along. If you wish, the class can repeat chorally.

■ Complete the information in the activity with your own answers. Tell the class. Students then work alone to give their own answers.

■ Students compare their answers with a partner.

■ Ask a few of the students to share their responses with the class.

Alternative presentation

■ As a warm-up, students make name tags for themselves like the one on page 2 of their books. Use the name tags to illustrate the meaning of "name," "female," and "male." Then read the Snapshot aloud to the class.

Optional activities

1. If appropriate, ask students to supply native language equivalents for some of the English names in the Snapshot. Ask, for example, "What's the name 'Katherine' in your language?"

2. In a homogeneous class, students work in small groups to make a list of first names from their native country. In a heterogeneous class, each student in the group can contribute two or three names from his or her country. Compare results as a class. Use a map to show where different names come from, if necessary.

2 CONVERSATION 🔊

SB p. 2 This activity presents conversational expressions for introducing yourself and asking for clarification. It also introduces possessive pronouns.

■ Books open. Play the tape several times as students listen only.

■ Read the conversation sentence by sentence. The class repeats each sentence after you say it. If necessary, break the longer sentences into shorter phrases. Explain that in the conversation "I'm sorry" = "I don't understand."

■ Look at the picture. Explain that it is common in North America to shake hands when you meet someone. Illustrate this with a student by introducing yourself and shaking hands.

■ Students practice the conversation in pairs, using the Look Up and Say technique. That is, students look briefly at a sentence in their book and then look up at their partner and say the sentence.

■ Circulate around the class and give help with pronunciation and intonation.

■ Ask for volunteers to perform the conversation for the rest of the class.

3 THE ALPHABET 🔊

SB p. 2 This exercise presents the alphabet and offers practice in spelling names.

1

■ Books open. Play the tape. Students repeat the letters of the alphabet chorally. Practice any sounds that are particularly difficult for your students.

■ Optional: In pairs, students say the alphabet twice, alternating back and forth between letters. Student A starts the first time, Student B the second time.

2 Pair work

■ Write your family name on the board, and spell it aloud for the class. Ask a few students to spell your name, and then their own name.

■ Students spell their own name for their partner. Then they take turns spelling their partner's name and your name.

Extra practice

■ Students practice the conversation in exercise 2 again, this time substituting their own information for that of Michael and Jennifer. If necessary, write the conversation on the board, leaving blanks where students' own names go. Students take turns going first, then switch partners.

Optional activity: *Family names*

■ Students make a complete list of their classmates' family names by moving around the classroom, using the conversation in exercise 2 as a model. They write down the names as they are spelled. (10 minutes)

---

4 GRAMMAR FOCUS: *my, your, his, her* 🔲

SB p. 3 The Grammar Focus presents the possessive adjectives *my, your, his,* and *her* in questions and answers about names. It also introduces the contraction *what's.*

> **Grammar note**
>
> *My, your, his,* and *her* are adjectives that indicate possession. They always come before the noun or noun phrase they modify.

■ Books open. Students look at the pictures of Jennifer and read what she says.

■ Demonstrate the use of *my, his,* and *her* by asking two students to come up and stand on either side of you. With appropriate gestures say: "My name is X. His name is Y. Her name is Z."

■ Use the tape to present the questions and answers in the box. Students listen and repeat.

■ Model *what's* and *what is.* Explain that *what's* is a "contraction" (or "reduced form") of *what is. What's* is for speaking, and *what is* is for writing. Practice the pronunciation of *what's* until students feel comfortable.

Group work: "The Name Game"

■ If the class is small enough, have the entire class form a single circle to play "The Name Game." In a large class, break up into groups of eight to ten.

■ Explain the game by modeling the example in the book. If necessary, demonstrate the game with a small group.

■ Students play the game, going around the circle at least twice. Join a group and play yourself, or circulate to keep students on task.

■ If time permits, one volunteer from each group gives the names of all the other students in the group.

Extra practice

■ Follow up the activity with a class quiz on names. Write the following on the board:

_____ *name is* _____ .

■ Point to one student and ask the class: "What's her (his) name?" Students write down the answer.

■ Select another student and ask again: "What's his (her) name?" Students write down the answer.

■ Continue like this with several more students. Then check the answers as a class by asking the same students "What's your name?" and having those students respond aloud. (10 minutes)

5] LISTENING 🔲

SB p. 3 This activity practices understanding names spelled aloud.

1

■ Books open. Students look at the photos. Ask: "What's her (his) name?" (It does not matter if students do not recognize the people in the photos.)

■ Explain the task: Students listen to a conversation about these people. They write down the last name (family name).

■ Play the tape. The first time students listen only and do not write. Reassure students that they do not have to understand every word they hear in order to do the task.

■ Play the tape for photo (a) only. Students write the answer. If necessary, play the tape for (a) several times. Then repeat the process for (b) and (c).

2   Pair work

■ Books open. Explain the task: Students check their answers to the listening activity by asking about each person in the photos. Model the dialogue with a student.

■ Students work in pairs.

■ Check answers around the class, and have selected students write them on the board.

■ Finally, repeat the entire recording so that students can check their answers again.

Tape transcript

1 Who are they? Listen to the conversations. Spell their last names.

a)
A: Who is this?
B: It's Whitney Houston.
A: Oh, right. She's a singer. Hm. How do you spell "Houston"?
B: It's H–O–U–S–T–O–N.

b)
A: And who is this man?
B: That's Jackie Chan, the movie star.
A: Chan or Chang?
B: Chan. C–H–A–N.

c)
A: I know this person. He's a film director.
B: Right. His first name is Steven, but what's his last name?
A: Spielberg.
B: How do you spell it?
A: S–P–I–E–L–B–E–R–G.

Answers

a) Houston
b) Chan
c) Spielberg

Extra practice

■ Bring photos of some other famous people to class. Hold up the photos one at a time, explain who the person is, and dictate the spelling of the person's name.

■ Students listen and write down the names they hear, and then check with a partner before you provide the answers. (5 minutes)

6 CONVERSATION 🔲

SB p. 4 This conversation presents the verb *be* in statements and questions, and practices possessive pronouns.

- Books open. Play the tape as students listen and read. Use the illustration to help explain the context.

- Model the conversation sentence by sentence; the class repeats. Use gestures to show that "excuse me" is used to get someone's attention.

- Put students into groups of three to practice the conversation. Encourage them to use the Look Up and Say technique. Circulate to help with pronunciation.

- If you wish, have two or three groups perform the conversation for the class.

Extra practice

- Have groups of three substitute their own names in the conversation and act it out using a book as a prop.

7 GRAMMAR FOCUS: The verb *be* 🔲

SB p. 4 The Grammar Focus presents the verb *be* in question and statement forms, as well as in reduced forms (contractions).

- Books open. Use the tape to present the information in the box. Students read as they listen. Play the tape again; this time students listen and repeat.

- Contrast the pronunciation of *I am* and *I'm, you are* and *you're,* and so on. Contractions of *be* are in statements, not in questions.

- Check comprehension by making a few true and false sentences about the class with *be:* "My name is (name). She's (name). This is her book." Students listen and say "true" or "false."

1

- Students read the conversations silently and fill in the blanks with correct forms of *be*.

- Students compare answers with a partner or as a class. Then they practice the conversations in pairs.

Answers

Nicole: Excuse me, <u>are</u> you Steven Carlson?
David: No, <u>I'm</u> not. <u>He's</u> over there. My name <u>is</u> David Bloom.
Nicole: Thanks, David.

Nicole: Are you Steven Carlson?
Steven: Yes, I <u>am</u>.
Nicole: <u>I'm</u> Nicole Johnson.
Steven: <u>It's</u> nice to meet you. I think <u>you're</u> in my math class.
Nicole: Yes, I <u>am</u>. And I think this <u>is</u> your book.
Steven: Yes, <u>it's</u> my math workbook. My name <u>is</u> here. Thank you!

2 Class activity

- Books open. Explain the task: Each student writes his or her name on a piece of paper and puts it in a pile. (You can pile the pieces of paper on a desk, or collect them in a hat or container.)

- Model the task: Take a slip of paper from the pile and ask: "Excuse me, are you _____?" Then each student draws a slip of paper and finds the person by asking questions.

8 | NUMBERS 🔘

SB p. 5 This exercise introduces the numbers zero through ten.

1

■ Books open. Play the tape as students listen and read. Then play it again as students repeat chorally.

2

■ Students work in pairs and take turns saying the numbers on the cards in the illustration. Check answers by calling on students to say the numbers for the class.

■ Explain that 9067 = nine-zero-six-seven *or* nine-oh-six-seven. Both are correct.

3   Group work

■ Model the example by calling on a student. Ask: "What's your telephone number?"

■ Students work in groups of four or five. They take turns asking each other's phone numbers. Each student writes down the numbers to form a group list. Students can make up a number if they do not want to give their actual phone numbers.

■ Students in each group compare lists to see if they heard each number correctly.

Extra practice

■ Students work alone and write three important numbers on a piece of paper. For example, they can write their house number, a friend's phone number, or they can make up a number.

■ Students work in pairs and read aloud each others' numbers. (5 minutes)

INTERCHANGE 1:
Directory assistance

SB pp. IC-2 and IC-4 This is an information-gap activity that practices spelling names and giving telephone numbers. The emphasis is on communication.

1   Role play

■ Students work in pairs as Student A and Student B. All of the A's look at page IC-2, and all of the B's look at page IC-4. Students do not look at their partner's information.

■ Explain the situation: Student A needs telephone numbers. For example, what is the phone number for Ms. Kumiko Roku? Student A phones the operator to find out. Student B is the operator and gives the numbers.

■ Model the sample conversation with a student. If the class needs more help getting started, do one or two names on the list as a class.

■ Students do the activity in pairs.

2

■ Pairs change roles: Student A becomes the operator and B is the customer.

■ At the end of the entire activity, compare answers as a class.

9 | LISTENING 🔘

SB p. 5 This activity practices listening to and writing down telephone numbers.

■ Books open. Use the picture to explain the situation: Victor wants the telephone numbers of students in his class. He asks Sarah Smith for the numbers.

■ Look at the list of names and model these for the class.

■ Play the tape. Students write down the phone numbers as they listen. Play the tape several times.

■ Ask students to compare answers with a partner. Then go over the answers with the class.

Tape transcript

Victor is making a list of telephone numbers of students in his class. He's talking to Sarah Smith. Listen and write the numbers.

VICTOR: OK. David Bloom. What's his telephone number?

SARAH: Let's see. David Bloom. His number is five-five-five, one-nine-three-seven.

VICTOR: Five-five-five, one-nine-three-seven?

SARAH: That's right.

SARAH: What about Steven Carlson?

VICTOR: I have Steven's number. It's five-five-five, nine-one-seven-three.

SARAH: And Nicole Johnson?

VICTOR: Yes, Nicole. What's her number?

SARAH: It's five-five-five, eight-four-one-two.

VICTOR: Five-five-five, eight-four-one-two.

VICTOR: OK. And what about Lisa Liu?

Sarah: Her number is five-five-five, three-eight-six-oh.

VICTOR: Three-six-eight-oh?

SARAH: No, three-eight-six-oh.

VICTOR: OK, and Michael Lynch?

SARAH: His number is five-five-five, two-eight-seven-one.

VICTOR: And Brian Noguchi's number?

SARAH: His number is five-five-five, seven-four-eight-two.

VICTOR: Let's see. Jennifer Wan. Is her number five-five-five, two-nine-four-seven?

SARAH: Yeah, that's right.

VICTOR: By the way, what's your telephone number, Sarah?

SARAH: It's five-five-five, three-eight-oh-six.

VICTOR: OK. Thank you very much.

Answers

David Bloom	555-1937
Nicole Johnson	555-8412
Lisa Liu	555-3860
Michael Lynch	555-2871
Brian Noguchi	555-7482
Sarah Smith	555-3806

10 WORD POWER 🔈

SB p. 6 This vocabulary activity presents the English words for objects commonly found in classrooms. It introduces the indefinite articles *a* and *an*.

Note: An is used before words that begin with a vowel sound, and *a* is used before a consonant sound.

1

■ Books open. Play the tape as students look at the six illustrations. Students fill in the blanks with *a* or *an* as they listen. Play the tape as many times as necessary.

■ Students compare answers with a partner or as a class.

Tape transcript with answers

a) This is a book.
b) This is an English book.
c) This is a notebook.
d) This is an eraser.
e) This is a dictionary.
f) This is an umbrella.

2

■ Books open. Explain the task: Students look at the words in the box. Are these things in the classroom?

■ Students silently look about the room and check off the items as they find them. If they don't know a word, they circle it.

■ Ask if there are any words the students didn't know. If so, point out the objects in the classroom.

■ Model the dialogue. Then students practice in pairs.

■ Pairs move about the room, pointing at objects as they identify them.

■ Bring the class back together, and ask several students to identify an object and spell its name for the class.

11 GREETINGS AND TITLES 🔄

SB p. 6 This activity introduces titles used with last names, common greetings, and ways to say good-bye.

Note: You may want to do this activity at the end of class.

1

■ Books open. Play the tape. Students listen and repeat. (*Note:* The tape models not only the list of expressions, but the dialogue in the illustrations as well.)

■ Explain that titles are used with last names (family names) only and that using titles makes greetings more formal. Give students these examples to contrast formal and informal:

Formal: greeting a teacher
Informal: greeting a friend

■ Lead choral and individual repetition of the greetings and ways to say good-bye, both with and without titles.

■ Look at the illustration. Remind students that in North America people often shake hands when they greet each other. When people say good-bye, they often wave their hand.

2

■ Students stand up and move around the class, greeting each other and then saying good-bye. If you wish, they can shake hands and wave as well.

12 INSTRUCTIONS 🔄

SB p. 7 This activity presents affirmative imperatives that are common in classrooms.

1

■ Books open. Play the tape as students listen and read. Repeat if necessary.

■ Rewind and play the tape again. This time, students perform the actions as they listen. (The first action is to close their books; they should try to follow the instructions without reading as they listen. If this is too difficult, have them open their books again and continue.)

2 Class activity

■ Books closed. Tell students: "Listen and do." Give instructions like those in the book, making them appropriate to your setting. Students perform the actions as a class or individually. Use vocabulary words from exercise 10 as well.

3 Pair work

■ Students work alone to write six instructions similar to those presented in parts 1 and 2 above. Circulate to provide help and check accuracy.

■ In pairs, Student A says his or her instructions, and Student B performs the actions. Then Student B says his or her instructions.

2 What's this called in English?

This unit has two cycles and presents the language needed to talk about objects that people carry with them. It focuses on singular and plural nouns, *this* and *these*, possessives, yes/no questions, and prepositions of place.

UNIT PLAN

Cycle 1

1 Snapshot: *Introduces names of common objects that people carry with them*

2 Spelling and Pronunciation: *Presents the different ways that plural* s *is pronounced*

3 Conversation: *Practices asking the names of objects and introduces* this/these

4 Grammar Focus: *Practices singular and plural nouns with* this *and* these

5 Conversation: *Introduces yes/no questions with* be *and possessives*

6 Grammar Focus: *Presents possessives and yes/no questions with* be

7 Listening: *Practices listening for possessives*

WORKBOOK: Exercises 1–4 on pages 5 to 7

Cycle 2

8 Conversation: *Introduces prepositions of place and questions with* where

9 Prepositions of Place: *Presents* in, on, under, next to, behind, *and* in front of

10 Lost Items: *A fluency activity that reviews prepositions of place and the vocabulary of common objects*

Interchange 2: *A pair work activity that reviews the grammar and vocabulary of the unit*

11 Instructions: *Reviews imperatives, possessives, prepositions, and vocabulary of common objects*

WORKBOOK: Exercise 5 on page 8

ng   *th=they*

1 SNAPSHOT

SB p. 8 This exercise builds interest in the topic of the unit and introduces essential vocabulary.

■ Books closed. Show the class some of the things you carry in your bag or briefcase. As you pull each item out, ask the class: "What is this called in English?" Students call out the answers. If they do not know, supply the English word.

■ On the board, write:

Things people carry	
1. money	5.
2. photos	6.
3.	7.
4.	8.

Ask the class to name six other things that people carry. Write these on the board.

■ Books open. Students read the Snapshot. Ask them to write a check mark next to the items that are on the board.

■ Ask students to call out the items in the Snapshot that are not listed on the board. Add these to the list.

■ Students do the task individually: They make a list of the things they are carrying with them today.

■ Students compare answers with a partner. Help with vocabulary if necessary.

■ Take a poll to see what students carry. What are the most common things? The least common?

2 SPELLING AND PRONUNCIATION: Plurals 🔲

SB p. 8 This exercise introduces the three different ways of pronouncing plural *s*. These are the rules:

1. When nouns end in the sibilant sounds /s/, /z/, /ʃ/, /tʃ/, /ʒ/, or /dʒ/, the plural takes an extra syllable /ɪz/ (e.g., glass – glasses).

j = jam

2. After nouns ending in a vowel sound and after other voiced consonants, *s* is pronounced /z/ (e.g., pen – pens). Voiced consonants: /b/, /d/, /g/, /l/, /m/, /n/, /ŋ/, /r/, /ð/, and /v/.

3. After other unvoiced final consonants, *s* is pronounced /s/ (e.g., book – books). Unvoiced consonants: /p/, /t/, /k/, /f/, and /θ/. — *th = thin*

■ Books open. Play the tape to introduce the sounds. Students listen and read.

■ Lead choral and individual repetition of each sound and the corresponding word list.

■ If students have trouble distinguishing between /s/ and /z/, ask them to put a hand over their throat. Explain that the throat moves or buzzes for /z/ but not for /s/.

Extra practice

■ List these words on the board: comb, purse, notebook, photo, tissue. Students work in pairs to form the plural for each, and then sort the words into the correct column.

Answers

s = /s/	s = /z/	s = /ɪz/
notebooks	combs	purses
	photos	
	tissues	

■ If you wish, have pairs think of one additional word to add to each column. (5 minutes)

3 CONVERSATION 🔲

SB p. 8 This conversation presents expressions for asking what things are called in English, and introduces the demonstrative pronouns *this* and *these*.

■ Books open. Play the tape as students listen and read.

■ Explain *this* by using classroom objects: "*This* is the board. *This* is a book. *This* is a pen." Explain *these* in the same way: "*These* are pens." (etc.). Show the difference between *this* and *these* by holding up first one pen and then two or more: "*This* is a pen. *These* are pens."

■ Read the conversation sentence by sentence; the class repeats. Use the picture to give the meaning of "sunglasses."

■ In pairs, students practice the conversation using the Look Up and Say technique.

■ If you wish, have several pairs read or act out the conversation for the class.

4 GRAMMAR FOCUS: *this, these;* singular and plural nouns

SB p. 9 The Grammar Focus presents the demonstrative pronouns *this* and *these* with singular and plural nouns. It also reviews *a* and *an* (see Unit 1, ex. 10).

■ Books open. Play the tape as students listen and read the sentences in the box.

■ Demonstrate singular and plural with other objects until students understand the difference.

■ If necessary, point out that *a/an* are used with singular nouns only. They are never used with plural nouns.

1

■ Explain the task: Students look at the pictures. Ask: "What's this called in English?" They write the answer. As students work, circulate to provide help as needed.

■ Have students compare answers with a partner. Then play the tape and check answers as a class.

■ Play the tape again, or model the sentences yourself. Students repeat each sentence chorally.

Tape transcript with answers

a) This is an umbrella.
b) These are glasses.
c) This is a calculator.
d) This is a handbag.
e) This is a briefcase.
f) These are tissues.
g) This is a newspaper.
h) These are photos.
i) This is an address book.

2 Pair work

■ Model the task by placing four objects on a desk and covering them with a piece of paper. Model the conversation alone or with a student.

■ In pairs, students take turns guessing the items their partner has covered up. (If the items are too large to cover with a piece of paper, students could alternatively close their eyes and touch the objects, then guess what the object is.)

■ Ask for volunteers to hold up one of their partner's items and tell the class what it is.

5 CONVERSATION

SB p. 10 This conversation presents expressions for asking about ownership and introduces possessives and yes/no questions with *be*.

■ Books open. As a class, look at the illustration. Ask: "What are the people talking about?" (Answer: the umbrella)

■ Play the tape as students listen and read.

■ Model the conversation sentence by sentence. The class repeats chorally. Demonstrate "excuse me" (used to get someone's attention) by saying it as you tap on a student's shoulder. Demonstrate "let me see" by saying it as you hold up something (preferably an umbrella) and examine it closely.

■ In groups of three, students practice the conversation using the Look Up and Say technique. Have groups say the conversation three times so that each student has a chance to practice all the sentences.

■ If you wish, have several groups say their conversation for the class.

Extra practice

■ Groups act out the conversation by substituting their own names and a different item. If necessary, write the conversation on the board with blanks for the students to fill in with their own information.

6 GRAMMAR FOCUS:
Possessives; yes/no questions with *be* ▭

SB pp. 10–11 The Grammar Focus presents possessive adjectives (*my, your,* etc.), the possessive case of proper names (*'s*), and yes/no questions with *be*.

■ Books open. Play the tape as students read the sentences in the boxes.

■ Model each sentence. The class repeats. Pay particular attention to the pronunciation of the possessive *'s*. *Note:* When *'s* follows a person's name, apply the same pronunciation rules as for plural nouns:

1. When a name ends with the sounds /s/, /z/, /ʃ/, /tʃ/, /ʒ/, or /dʒ/, it takes an extra syllable /ɪz/ (e.g., Alice – Alice's, James – James's).
2. If a name ends with a vowel sound or other voiced consonant, *s* is pronounced /z/ (e.g., Daniel – Daniel's, Sarah – Sarah's, Tom – Tom's).
3. When a name ends with an unvoiced consonant, *s* is pronounced /s/ (e.g., Robert – Robert's).

1

■ Students work individually to fill in the blanks in the conversations.

■ Students compare their answers in pairs. Then check answers as a class.

■ Model the conversations; students repeat each sentence chorally. Then students practice the conversations in pairs.

Answers

A: Is this your calculator?
B: No, it's not. My calculator is different.

A: Are these Jennifer's sunglasses?
B: No, they're not. Maybe they're Nicole's.

A: Mr. and Mrs. Lee, is your telephone number 555-1287?
B: No, our number is 555-2287.

A: Is this Lisa's address book?
B: Yes, it is. Her name is right here.

A: Are these your keys?
B: Yes, they are. Thank you very much.

A: Is this your newspaper?
B: Let me see. No, it's not. It's Michael's. His name and address are here.

2 Pair work

■ Books open. As students look at the six photos, ask: "What is this called? / What are these called?" Students respond: "This is a newspaper." (etc.).

■ Explain the task by modeling the example dialogue with a student. Then students do the task in pairs. Students can take turns asking and answering, or pairs can do the exercise twice: the first time with Student A asking, and the second time with Student A answering.

■ If you wish, pairs can share one of their questions and answers with the class.

3 Group work

■ Arrange students in small groups. Each group has a bag, a small box, or an envelope to put things in.

■ Books open. Explain the task: Each person in the group puts one thing in the bag/box/envelope. Model the conversation for the class with one of the groups.

■ Students take turns asking about the items they select.

■ Circulate, paying particular attention to pronunciation. Review any problems at the end as a class.

7 LISTENING ▭

SB p. 11 This activity practices listening for key information.

■ Books open. Ask students to name the objects in the illustration. Then set the context for the tape: Sarah is talking with her classmates: Jennifer, Michael, Nicole, and Steven. She is cleaning up the classroom. She wants to know: Who owns the things in the picture? Refer to the chart as you explain.

- Play the tape. Students listen only and do not write. Play the tape again; this time students check the names on the chart as they listen. Play the tape several times, as necessary.

- Students compare answers with a partner or around the class.

Tape transcript

Sarah is cleaning up the classroom. Who owns these things? Listen and check the right name.

SARAH: Jennifer, is this your calculator?
JENNIFER: No, it's not. I think it's Michael's. Michael, is this your calculator?
MICHAEL: Yes, it is. Thanks.
SARAH: And are these your sunglasses, Jennifer?
JENNIFER: No, they're Nicole's, I think.
SARAH: Nicole, are these your sunglasses?
NICOLE: Hm. Yes, they are. Thank you, Sarah.
SARAH: And the book bag is Steven's, right? Steven, here . . . take your book bag.
STEVEN: OK. Thanks.
SARAH: And what about this hairbrush?
MICHAEL: Hm. Let me see. I think the hairbrush is Jennifer's. Jennifer?
JENNIFER: Yes, it's my hairbrush.

Answers

calculator: Michael
sunglasses: Nicole
book bag: Steven
hairbrush: Jennifer

8 CONVERSATION

SB p. 12 This conversation introduces prepositions of place and *where* questions with *be*.

- Books open. Students cover the conversation with a piece of paper and look at the picture. Set the scene: Katherine is watching the Brown family's baby. Mr. Brown is telling Katherine where things are in his house.

- Books closed. On the board write: "Where is the baby?" Ask students to listen for the answer.

- Play the tape once or twice. Ask students where the baby is.

- Books open. Play the tape again as students read and listen.

- Read the conversation line by line. Students repeat chorally. Use the illustration to explain new vocabulary (e.g., cabinet, television) and prepositions.

- In pairs, students practice the conversation using the Look Up and Say technique.

- If you wish, ask pairs to perform for the class.

9 PREPOSITIONS OF PLACE

SB p. 12 This exercise presents and practices prepositions of place.

- Books open. Students look at the six pictures illustrating prepositions of place. Play the tape or model the prepositions. Students repeat.

- Model each preposition like this: "The keys are in the bag." Students repeat.

- Use objects in the classroom to give more examples. For example, put an eraser under a book and ask: "Where is the eraser?"

- Students work individually to complete the sentences.

- Students compare answers with a partner and then check them as a class as they listen to the tape.

Tape transcript with answers

a) The briefcase is in front of the television.
b) The keys are in the handbag.
c) The wallet is under the newspaper.
d) The umbrella is behind the wastebasket.
e) The comb is next to the hairbrush.
f) The notebooks are on the dictionary.

10 LOST ITEMS

SB p. 13 This fluency activity provides further practice with prepositions of place.

■ Books open. Ask students a few questions about the picture, for example: "What's on the chair? What's under the table?"

Pair work

■ Explain the task: Students use the picture to answer the questions.

■ Working in pairs, students take turns answering and asking the questions:

A: Where is my briefcase?
B: It's in front of the chair (next to the table).

■ When pairs have finished, ask the questions around the class to check answers.

Answers

a) It's in front of the chair (next to the table).
b) It's on the chair.
c) They're under the table (on the floor).
d) It's on the table (next to the newspaper).
e) It's in your pocket.
f) They're in the briefcase.
g) It's behind the chair (next to the door).

Extra practice

■ Working individually, students draw a scene similar to the one in exercise 10.

■ Students exchange drawings with a partner, and then take turns asking and answering questions about the location of the things in each other's drawing. (10 minutes)

INTERCHANGE 2:
Find the differences

SB p. IC-3 This extension activity reviews prepositions of place, plurals, and *where* questions with *be*.

1 Pair work

■ Books open to page IC-3. Show the class the two pictures, A and B. Pointing to picture A, ask: "Where is the newspaper?" Then answer: "In picture A, it's on the bed." Pointing to picture B, ask: "Where is the newspaper?" Then answer: "In picture B, it's next to the bed" (*or* "on the floor," etc.).

■ Ask the class: "Where are the sunglasses?" Students respond. (Answer: In picture A, they're on the television. In picture B, they're behind the television.)

■ In pairs, students take turns asking and answering questions until they find all the differences in the two illustrations.

2 Class activity

■ Talk about the differences in the pictures as a class. Ask: "Where is the newspaper?" Students use the example in the book to answer: "In picture A, the newspaper is on the bed. In picture B, it's on the floor (next to the bed)." Ask about all the items in the picture, going around the class so that everyone has a chance to answer.

Sample answers

The following answers give the different locations of items in pictures A and B.

sunglasses
picture A: on the television
picture B: behind the television

newspaper
A: on the bed
B: next to the bed / in front of the books / on the floor

pens/pencils
A: on the book
B: next to the book

hairbrush
A: on the chair
B: in front of the chair / on the floor

briefcase
A: on the desk
B: on the chair

keys
A: on the desk / next to the briefcase
B: next to the chair / in front of the desk /
   on the floor

umbrella
A: behind the wastebasket
B: next to the wastebasket

cassette player
A: on the table
B: under the bed / on the floor

photos
A: on the table / next to the cassette player
B: in front of the table / on the floor

Extra practice

■ Make false statements about objects in the classroom. Students correct you:

Teacher: The eraser is in the wastebasket.
Student: No, it's on the desk.

11 INSTRUCTIONS

SB p. 13 This activity practices imperatives containing prepositions of place.

1

■ Books open. Play the tape as students listen and read.

■ Books closed. Tell students to clear their desks. Play the tape again. Students follow the instructions they hear.

2   Pair work

■ Tell students to write their own instructions using prepositions. Give them a few minutes to do this. Write one instruction as a class to get started, if necessary.

■ In pairs, students take turns giving and following each other's instructions.

■ Pairs of volunteers can give and follow instructions for the class. Alternatively, individual students can give the entire class an instruction to follow.

Extra practice

■ In small groups, students write five "silly" instructions, such as "Put your notebook on your head."

■ Groups read their instructions to the class, and the class follows them.

■ After all groups have led the class, the class votes on the silliest instruction. (10 minutes)

3 Where are you from?

This unit has two cycles and introduces language for talking about countries, nationalities, and languages. It also focuses on statements with *be*, and questions and short answers with *be*.

UNIT PLAN

Cycle 1

1 Snapshot: *Introduces the topic of countries and regions*

2 Word Power: *Extends the vocabulary of country names*

3 Conversation: *Introduces asking and answering about one's own country*

4 Grammar Focus: *Practices affirmative and negative statements with* be *using contractions*

WORKBOOK: Exercises 1–3 on pages 9 and 10

Cycle 2

5 Conversation: *Introduces the topics of nationalities and languages*

6 Countries and Nationalities: *Practices countries and nationalities with attention to syllable stress*

7 Languages: *A vocabulary-building exercise*

8 Listening: *Practices listening for countries, nationalities, and languages*

9 Grammar Focus: *Practices questions and short answers with* be

Interchange 3: *Reviews and practices names of countries*

WORKBOOK: Exercises 4–7 on pages 11 and 12

1 SNAPSHOT

`SB p. 14` This exercise introduces the theme of the unit – countries and nationalities – with some statistics on immigration.

■ Books closed. Ask if anyone knows what an immigrant is. (Perhaps there are some immigrants in the class.) For example, a person from another country who comes to the U.S. to live is an immigrant. Use a map as a visual aid.

■ Write the following on the board:

Immigrants to the U.S. (1970–1990)

_____ *Korea*
_____ *Mexico*
_____ *China*
_____ *the Philippines*
_____ *India*
_____ *Cuba*
_____ *Vietnam*

Say: "Some people from these countries live in the U.S. now. They are immigrants."

■ Ask: "Which country has the most immigrants to the U.S.?" Students work in pairs and rank the seven countries.

■ Pairs share their guesses with the rest of the class. List these guesses on the board.

■ Books open. Students read the Snapshot silently. Then they compare the information with their own answers. Discuss their findings as a class.

■ Students do the task individually.

■ Students compare their answers with a partner or around the class.

2 WORD POWER

`SB p. 14` This activity builds students' vocabulary of country names.

■ Model the name of each region. Students point to the area on the Snapshot map as they repeat.

■ Form groups of four or five. Group members work together to list two other countries for each region. (Alternatively, you can do this as a class.)

■ Each group reports to the class the countries they have listed. List these on the board; students can copy down names they do not know.

■ If you wish, model the country names and practice their pronunciation.

3 CONVERSATION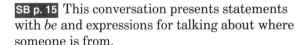

`SB p. 15` This conversation presents statements with *be* and expressions for talking about where someone is from.

1

■ Books open. Set the scene by telling students to look at the picture. Say: "Mark is talking to Laura. He's asking what country she's from. Listen."

■ Play the tape. Students listen and read.

■ Present the conversation line by line; students repeat. Explain or demonstrate the following:

originally = at first; in the beginning
actually = politely introduces a correction
Oh, right = Yes (agreement)

■ Students practice the conversation in pairs using the Look Up and Say technique.

■ If you wish, have several pairs act out the conversation for the class.

(instructions continue on next page)

2

■ Say: "Now listen to the rest of the conversation. Listen for the answers to these questions: Where is Mark from? Where is his country?"

■ Play the rest of the conversation at least twice. Students listen and write the answers.

■ Students compare answers in pairs before you go over them with the class.

Tape transcript for part 2

2 Listen to the rest of the conversation. a) Where is Mark from? b) Where is his country?

LAURA: How about you, Mark? Where are you from?
MARK: Guess. But I'm not from the United States.
LAURA: Oh, then are you from England?
MARK: No, I'm not.
LAURA: Maybe Canada. Are you from Canada?
MARK: No, I'm not from Canada. Actually, I'm from New Zealand.
LAURA: New Zealand? New Zealand is in the Pacific, right?
MARK: Yes, it's near Australia.
LAURA: Oh, yes. New Zealand. The kiwi fruit is from there.
MARK: That's right.

Answers

a) Mark is from New Zealand.
b) His country is in the Pacific, near Australia.

4 GRAMMAR FOCUS: Statements with *be* 📼

SB pp. 15–16 The Grammar Focus presents affirmative and negative statements with *be* using contractions.

> **Grammar/pronunciation notes**
>
> 1. In negative sentences, *not* comes **after** the *be* verb, not before (as it does in Spanish, for example).
>
> 2. *He's not* and *He isn't* mean exactly the same thing and are interchangeable. However, nouns (as opposed to pronouns) are generally followed by *isn't* or *aren't* (e.g., Costa Rica *isn't* in South America. My keys *aren't* in my handbag.).
>
> 3. The pronunciation is the same for *your* and *you're*.

■ Books open. Play the tape or model the information in the box. Students read and listen.

■ Play the tape again; students repeat.

■ Elicit the full forms of the contractions from students (e.g., *You're = You are*; *You're not* and *You aren't = You are not*). Check that students understand how to form the contractions.

1 Pair work

■ Look at the model sentence as a class. Students work individually to complete the sentences. (If students have trouble, do two sentences together as a class.)

■ Have students compare their answers with a partner. Then go over the answers as a class.

Answers

b) My family is from Korea. We're in the U.S. now, but <u>we're not</u> / <u>we aren't</u> from the U.S. originally.

c) Your glasses are on the table. <u>They're</u> over there, next to the newspaper.

d) Hi, Sarah – oh, I'm sorry! <u>You're not</u> / <u>You aren't</u> Sarah. Your name is Susan.

e) <u>Where is</u> my driver's license? <u>It's not</u> / <u>It isn't</u> in my wallet! Where is it?

f) Katherine and I aren't in your class. <u>We're</u> in Mrs. Lee's class.

g) Mr. Ho isn't from Hong Kong. <u>He's</u> from Singapore.

2

■ Students complete the three conversations individually with the correct form of *be*. Circulate to provide help as needed.

■ Have students compare answers with a partner. Then go over the answers with the class by calling on pairs to perform the conversations.

Answers

A: Where <u>is</u> Laura Sánchez from – South America?
B: No, she <u>isn't</u> from South America. <u>She's</u> from Costa Rica.
A: Oh. So <u>she's</u> from Central America.

A: Keiko, where <u>are</u> you and Kenji from?
B: <u>We're</u> both from Japan.
A: Oh, <u>are</u> you from Tokyo?
B: No, <u>we</u> <u>aren't</u> from Tokyo. <u>We're</u> from Kyoto.

A: Where <u>are</u> you from, Mr. Park?
B: <u>I'm</u> from the city of Pusan.
A: Where <u>is</u> Pusan, exactly? My geography <u>isn't</u> very good.
B: Pusan <u>is</u> in Korea.

Extra practice

■ In pairs, students write a conversation similar to the last dialogue in exercise 4, substituting their own information for that of Mr. Park. Students practice their conversations.

■ If you wish, ask pairs to act out their conversation for the class.

5 CONVERSATION

SB p. 16 This conversation presents expressions for asking and talking about language and nationality.

■ Books open. Set the scene by looking at the picture. Ask the class questions: "What is the man giving the woman? Is the newspaper in English? What language is this? Where do people speak Spanish?"

■ Play the tape. Students listen and read.

■ Present the conversation line by line; students repeat.

■ Students practice the conversation in pairs using the Look Up and Say technique. Partners take turns playing Jack and Marta.

■ If you wish, ask several pairs to act out the conversation for the class.

6 COUNTRIES AND NATIONALITIES

SB p. 17 This activity presents names of countries and nationalities, and practices stress and intonation.

■ Play the tape as students read the sentences in the box. Play the tape again; students repeat.

■ Give more examples of nationalities by talking about people in the class: "I'm from (name of country). I'm (nationality). (*pointing to student*) Kenji is from Japan. He's Japanese."

1

■ Books closed. Write on the board: Mexico, Mexican, Korea, Korean. Explain that each of these words has three syllables. (A syllable is a word or part of a word that has more or less stress. Every syllable has a vowel.)

(instructions continue on next page)

■ Say "Mexico"; as you say it, tap the board under each syllable (Mex-i-co). Repeat this process with "Mexican" (Mex-i-can), "Korea" (Ko-re-a), and "Korean" (Ko-re-an). (*Note:* Don't worry about how to divide words into syllables; students should concentrate on *hearing* the words only.)

■ When students understand what a syllable is, introduce the concept of stress: Every word has a syllable that gets more emphasis than the others, for example: Mexico. The syllable with stress is louder and higher in pitch.

■ Say the words on the board (Mexican, Korea, Korean). As you say them, ask students which syllable gets the stress: 1, 2, or 3.

■ Books open. Play the tape or model the names of the countries and nationalities. Students listen and repeat each name.

■ Say the names again. This time when students repeat, they tap their hand on the desk as they say the stressed syllable (i.e., the syllable printed in bold). This will help illustrate where the stress is.

2

■ Explain the task: Students listen and underline the syllable with the most stress in each word.

■ Play the tape or model the words several times if necessary as students do the task.

■ Students compare answers with a partner.

■ Play the tape again to check answers. Students repeat each word and tap the desk as they say the stressed syllable.

Answers

Colombia	Colombian
Egypt	Egyptian
England	English
Italy	Italian
Poland	Polish
Lebanon	Lebanese
India	Indian
Cambodia	Cambodian
Turkey	Turkish
Venezuela	Venezuelan
Vietnam	Vietnamese
Peru	Peruvian

3 Pair work

■ If necessary, complete the first dialogue as a class so that students know what to do. Then students work in pairs to complete the conversations.

■ Pairs join together to compare their work. Then check answers around the class.

■ Model the conversations. Then have students practice them in pairs. Circulate and listen for correct stress.

Answers

(The stressed syllables are in bold here for reference.)

A: I'm from **Hun**gary.
B: Oh, so you're Hun**gar**ian.

A: Is Mr. Lee from Ko**rea**?
B: No, he's Chi**nese**. He's from **Chi**na.

A: Are you Vietna**mese**?
B: No, I'm not from Viet**nam**. I'm from Cam**bo**dia.

A: Your newspaper is in **Span**ish.
B: Yes, it's a **Span**ish newspaper. I'm from **Mex**ico.

A: We're from Pe**ru**.
B: Oh, so you're Pe**ru**vian.
A: That's right.

A: Are you from Ja**pan**?
B: Yes, we're Japa**nese**.

4 Class activity

■ Students guess the name of the country for each nationality listed.

Answers

(The stressed syllables are in bold here for reference.)

Ne**pal** – Nepa**lese**
Bo**li**via – Bo**li**vian
Panama – Pana**ma**nian
Indo**ne**sia – Indo**ne**sian
Cuba – **Cu**ban
Su**dan** – Suda**nese**
New **Zea**land – New **Zea**lander
France – **French**

7 LANGUAGES 🔊

SB p. 18 This activity presents names of
languages.

- Books closed. Write this list on the board.

The top 5 languages of the world
- ____ Spanish
- ____ Hindi
- ____ Chinese
- ____ English
- ____ Russian

- Students work in pairs or small groups to rank
these languages in order, from 1 to 5.

- If you wish, ask pairs or groups to try and list
the six official languages of the United Nations.

- Books open. Students read the information and
compare their answers with the information
given.

- Play the tape; students read the languages in
the boxes and repeat.

- Ask students for a country for each language.

- Students work individually to answer the two
questions, then share answers as a class. Explain
"official language" by giving examples: "In
Algeria, people speak French and Arabic, but
Arabic is the official language. In Malaysia, people
speak Chinese, Tamil, English, and Malay, but
Malay is the official language."

1 Class activity

- Students do the activity as a class. They say the
official language of the country and another
country with the same language (the language
does not have to be "official" in the other
country). They use the sample dialogue as a
model for their answers.

- List the country names and languages on the
board to see how many countries students can
name for each language.

Sample answers

a) German is the language of Austria. German is
the language of Germany / Switzerland, too.
b) Portuguese is the language of Brazil.
Portuguese is the language of Portugal, too. (It
is also spoken in some African countries, e.g.,
Mozambique, Angola.)
c) Spanish is the language of Chile. Spanish is the
language of Spain / Mexico / Argentina, too. (It
is spoken in most of Latin America except
Brazil.)
d) Arabic is the language of Morocco. Arabic is
the language of Egypt / Saudi Arabia / Oman /
Yemeni Republic / Kuwait / Syria, too. (It is
spoken in North Africa and the Middle East.)
e) English is the language of New Zealand.
English is the language of Australia / Canada /
the United States / the United Kingdom, too.
(It is also spoken in many other countries.)

2 Pair work

- Students look at the nine examples. Ask them:
"What do you think these languages are?" Model
the sample dialogue in the book, as well as
disagreement:

A: I think this is Italian.
B: No, I think it's Spanish.

Tell students that the point of the exercise is to
communicate with each other as they guess the
languages. They should not worry if they do not
know the answer.

- Students do the task in pairs.

- Pairs join together to compare answers before
you go over them as a class.

Answers

a) Spanish   e) Russian
b) French   f) German
c) Japanese   g) Portuguese
d) Chinese

8 LISTENING 🔊

SB p. 19 This activity practices listening for details about the speakers' country, nationality, and native language.

■ Books open. Explain the task: Students listen to three short conversations. Antonio, Mei-Ling, and Monique are talking about their country, nationality, and native language. If you wish, students can guess possible answers based on the people's names.

■ Play the tape once as students listen only.

■ Play the tape again; this time students complete the task as they listen. Play the tape several times if necessary. (If students have trouble, play and repeat each of the three short conversations separately.)

■ Students compare answers first with a partner, then as a class.

■ Play the tape a final time so that students can check their answers again.

Tape transcript

Antonio, Mei-Ling, and Monique meet for the first time. Where are they from? What are their native languages?

ANTONIO: Hi, my name's Antonio.
MEI-LING: Hi, I'm Mei-Ling.
ANTONIO: Nice to meet you, Mei-Ling.

MEI-LING: Where are you from?
ANTONIO: Well, I'm Brazilian.
MEI-LING: Oh, what part of Brazil are you from?
ANTONIO: I'm from Rio.
MEI-LING: So your native language is Spanish, right?
ANTONIO: Well, no, it's Portuguese.
MEI-LING: Oh, of course. They speak Portuguese in Brazil.

ANTONIO: Mei-Ling, is your name Chinese?
MEI-LING: Yes, it is. But I'm from the United States – from San Francisco.
ANTONIO: So you're American.
MEI-LING: Yes, I am. But my parents are from China originally.
ANTONIO: Is your native language Chinese?
MEI-LING: Yes, it is. We speak Chinese at home.

ANTONIO: By the way, Mei-Ling, this is Monique.
MEI-LING: Nice to meet you, Monique. Are you from Brazil, too?
MONIQUE: No, I'm from Canada.
MEI-LING: So you're Canadian. Is English your native language?
MONIQUE: No, it's French. I'm from Montreal.

Answers

Antonio: Brazil, Brazilian, Portuguese
Mei-Ling: the United States, American, Chinese
Monique: Canada, Canadian, French

9 GRAMMAR FOCUS: Questions and short answers with *be* 🔊

SB p. 19 The Grammar Focus practices questions with *be*, and affirmative and negative short answers.

Grammar note

Contracted forms are used only in negative short answers. Affirmative short answers are never contracted.

■ Books open. Play the tape or model the sentences in the box. Students listen and read.

■ Students practice the questions and answers chorally and in pairs.

■ Ask similar questions about classroom objects to make sure students understand how to form short answers. For example: "Am I from Korea? Are you from New Zealand? Is this a pen?"

1

■ Students work individually to match the questions and answers.

■ Students compare answers in pairs and then as a class.

■ Students practice the questions and answers in pairs.

Answers

a) 3   b) 6   c) 4   d) 1   e) 2   f) 5

2   Pair work

■ Explain the task: Students write five questions with *be*. They use the questions in part 1 as a model.

■ Students write their questions individually.

■ Circulate to provide help and check for accuracy.

■ In pairs, students take turns asking their questions. If you wish, when they are done, students change partners and ask their questions again.

INTERCHANGE 3:
Geography quiz

SB pp. IC-6 and IC-7 This activity provides an enjoyable and interesting review of countries, languages, and nationalities; questions and statements with *be*; and prepositions of place.

1   Pair work

■ Students open their books to pages IC-6 and IC-7.

■ Explain that students work together in pairs to answer the questions "Where are these countries? Where are these cities? Where are these monuments?"

■ Write these expressions on the board:

I think Taipei is in . . .
No, I think it's . . .
Maybe it's . . .
I don't know.

Tell students to use these expressions as they talk about the answers.

■ Students do the task. Tell them not to worry if they do not know the answers; the purpose is to communicate as they try to guess the answers.

2   Group work

■ When pairs have finished, they join another pair and compare answers. Then go over the answers as a class.

Answers

What are these countries?
a) Germany
b) Russia
c) New Zealand
d) Morocco (or Western Sahara/Mauritania)

Where are these cities?
a) China
b) Turkey
c) Taiwan
d) Kenya
e) Japan
f) New Zealand

Where are these monuments?
a) Egypt
b) India (city of Agra)
c) China
d) Greece (city of Athens)

Optional activity: *Guess the country*

■ Working individually, students think of a country and write clues, like this:

The language is Portuguese.
It's in Europe, next to Spain.
What country is it?
(Answer: Portugal)

■ Students form small groups and quiz their partners. Circulate to provide help as needed.

4 Clothes and weather

This unit has two cycles and presents vocabulary for talking about clothes and the weather, colors, and numbers from 11 to 100. It also focuses on the present continuous tense and coordinating conjunctions.

UNIT PLAN

Cycle 1

1 Snapshot: *Introduces the topic of clothes*

2 Colors: *A vocabulary-building exercise*

3 Word Power: *Builds and practices the vocabulary of clothes and colors*

4 Conversation: *Introduces talking about the weather in the present continuous*

5 Grammar Focus: *Practices the present continuous and the conjunctions* and, but, so

WORKBOOK: Exercises 1–4 on pages 13 to 15

Cycle 2

6 Numbers: *Presents numbers from 11 to 100*

7 Temperatures: *Fluency practice with numbers*

8 What's the Weather Like?: *Presents names of seasons and expressions for talking about the weather*

9 Listening: *Practices listening for specific information about the weather*

10 Clothes and Weather: *Reviews the vocabulary and grammar of the unit*

Interchange 4: *A fluency activity that reviews weather vocabulary, numbers, and country names*

WORKBOOK: Exercises 5–6 on pages 15 and 16

1 SNAPSHOT

SB p. 20 This exercise introduces the theme of clothes by giving some interesting facts about where various clothing items come from.

■ Books closed. Write this chart on the board:

Clothing	Country of origin
wristwatches	_____
blue jeans	_____
bathing suits	_____
neckties	_____
high heels	_____
pajamas	_____

India, France, Croatia, the United States, France, England

■ Say: "Wristwatches are originally from France." Write "France" next to the word "wristwatches" on the board.

■ Ask: "Where are these other clothes from originally?" Students work in pairs and guess the answers.

■ Ask several pairs to share their guesses with the class.

■ Books open. Students read the Snapshot and compare the information with their own answers. Explain that "19th century" = 1800s, and "17th century" = 1600s.

■ Answer the question in small groups or as a class. If students do not know the English word for an article of clothing from their own country, ask them to draw a picture of it on the board, then tell them the name in English.

■ In homogeneous classes, see how many articles of clothing students can list on the board from their country. In heterogeneous classes, write the names of countries on the board and the articles of clothing underneath.

2 COLORS 📼

SB p. 20 This exercise presents names of colors.

1

■ Books open. Play the tape. Students listen and repeat.

■ Practice the color names by pointing to objects around the room; students call out the color.

2 Pair work

■ Model the question in the Student's Book with a student. Then students do the task in pairs.

■ Take a class poll: Call on each student to name his or her favorite color and tally the results on the board.

Alternative presentation

■ As an alternative to pair work, do the following chain exercise: Ask a student his or her favorite color. The student answers and then asks the question to someone else, who answers and asks another student, and so on, around the class.

Optional activity: *Name that color*

■ Groups of eight to ten students sit in a circle. The first student holds up an object that he or she has brought to class. The next student says the color quickly: e.g., "blue" or "black." That student holds up another object. Continue like this around the circle, until someone makes a mistake or hesitates. Then begin again.

3 | WORD POWER: Clothes 🔲

SB pp. 21–22 This activity extends practice with colors and the vocabulary of clothing.

1

■ Books open. Model the names of clothes; students repeat.

■ Play the tape. Students follow in their books and repeat. If necessary, play the tape again.

■ Spot-check comprehension by pointing to similar items of clothing in the class; students say the color (e.g., "The shoes are black.").

Tape transcript

1 What color are these things? Listen and practice.

The suit is gray.
The blouse is white.
The skirt is dark green.
The dress is pink.
The slacks are light brown.
The shirt is light blue.
The tie is orange.
The coat is beige.
The shorts are white.
The running shoes are purple.
The hat is black.
The boots are green.
The scarf is yellow.
The T-shirt is red.
The shoes are gray.

2   Pair work

■ Explain the task and model the sample conversations with a student. Then have students talk about the clothes in the pictures in pairs.

■ Ask several students questions about the pictures, or conduct a chain drill as described in the alternative presentation for exercise 2 on page 37 of this Teacher's Manual.

3

■ As a class, look at the chart and the illustrations. Pick two items of clothing from pages 20 and 21 of the Student's Book, such as bathing suit and coat, and ask: "Is this for warm weather or for cold weather?" Students answer.

■ Then ask which list "hat" goes in. Some students may say warm weather (because it protects you from the sun), and some may say cold (because it keeps you warm). The students decide.

■ When students understand the task, they work in pairs. When they have filled the chart with words from their book, they add two more words to each list.

■ When it seems that most students have finished, have pairs form small groups to compare answers.

■ Call on students to share an answer with the class, and create a class list on the board. *Note:* Answers will vary depending on the part of the world students come from. Use disagreements as the basis of class discussion, or have the class vote on the "right" answer.

4 | CONVERSATION 🔲

SB p. 22 This conversation presents expressions for talking about the weather and introduces the present continuous.

■ Books open. Set the scene by looking at the picture. Ask questions: "Is it warm or cold weather? Is the woman cold?"

■ Play the tape as students listen and read.

■ Present the conversation line by line; students repeat. Explain or demonstrate that "uh-oh" = "oh no" (something is wrong), and that "Come on" = "Let's go" or "Let's do it now." Use the picture to define "snow," "thirty-two degrees," and "taxi."

■ Students practice the conversation in pairs using the Look Up and Say technique.

■ If you wish, ask pairs to act out the conversation for the class.

5 GRAMMAR FOCUS:
Present continuous; *and, but, so* 🔲

SB pp. 23–24 This Grammar Focus presents the present continuous tense and the conjunctions *and, but,* and *so.*

Grammar notes

1. The present continuous is used to talk about action in progress (what is happening now).

2. *And, but,* and *so* connect two sentences. *And* connects sentences of equal importance. *But* shows difference (contrast) between sentences. *So* shows the result of an action.

■ Books open. Play the tape or model the information in the present continuous box (left-hand box) only. Students read and repeat.

■ Then play the tape for the right-hand box; students repeat.

■ If necessary, demonstrate the meaning of *but* and *so* by writing these sentence stems on the board. Students complete them in pairs.

> *He's walking in the rain, so . . .*
> *He's walking in the rain, but . . .*
>
>> *. . . he's carrying an umbrella.*
>> *. . . he's not carrying an umbrella.*

1

■ Students work individually to match the first and second parts of sentences. They write the complete sentence on a sheet of paper.

■ Students compare answers with a partner and then check answers as a class by listening to the tape.

■ Point out the spelling of the continuous verb form (explained in the box in the lower right corner of page 23).

■ If you wish, call on students around the class to read a sentence.

Tape transcript with answers

a) She's running, so <u>she's wearing running shoes.</u> (3)
b) He's driving, but <u>he isn't wearing his glasses.</u> (6)
c) We're walking in the snow, but <u>we aren't wearing boots.</u> (2)
d) <u>She's swimming, and</u> she's wearing a green bathing suit. (5)
e) They're playing tennis, <u>but they aren't wearing tennis shoes.</u> (4)
f) <u>It's snowing, and</u> I'm taking a walk. (1)

2   Pair work

■ Students work in pairs to complete the sentences under each picture with the verbs in parentheses.

■ Pairs compare answers with another pair before you go over them as a class.

Answers

b) He's driving, and <u>she's running.</u>
c) It<u>'s snowing, and they're swimming.</u>
d) They<u>'re playing</u> basketball, so <u>they're wearing</u> shorts.
e) He<u>'s working</u> today, so <u>he's wearing</u> a suit and tie.
f) She<u>'s carrying</u> a briefcase, but she <u>isn't</u> (she<u>'s not</u>) <u>carrying</u> a handbag.

3   Class activity

■ Model the task by writing one true and one false sentence about yourself on the board, e.g.: "I'm wearing shoes. I'm wearing a hat." Read these to the class and ask if they are right or wrong. The class responds using the sample dialogue in their book.

■ Students work individually to write three true and three false sentences about what their classmates are wearing.

■ Circulate to help and check for accuracy.

■ Students take turns reading their sentences to the class. Their classmates say "That's right" or "That's wrong." They explain wrong answers with *but:* for example, "She's wearing shoes, but they aren't black (but they are brown)."

6 NUMBERS 🔲

SB p. 25 This exercise presents the numbers 11 through 100 (and beyond).

■ Books open. Play the tape or model the numbers. Students read and repeat.

■ For further practice, students work in pairs. Partners take turns saying a number; the other student points to the number on the page.

Extra practice

■ Make a circle. Starting with 11, each student says a number until they have counted to 100 (or higher). Students say the numbers as quickly as possible. (If you wish, start back at the beginning if anyone makes a mistake.)

Optional activity: *I'm thinking of a number . . .*

■ Books open to page 25. Students work in pairs. Each student circles three numbers between 11 and 100 but does not let his or her partner see.

■ Pairs take turns like this:

A: I'm thinking of a number between 11 and 20.
B: Is it 19?
A: No, it's not.
B: Is it 17?
A: Yes, it is.

---

7 TEMPERATURES

SB p. 25 This activity offers further practice with numbers by talking about temperatures.

■ Books closed. Write these words on the board:

temperature ⟨ *Celsius*
　　　　　　　 Fahrenheit

0 degrees Celsius = 32 degrees Fahrenheit

■ Ask questions to introduce the vocabulary. For example: "Is it warm or cold today? What's the temperature?" In a heterogeneous class, ask: "In your country, do you use Celsius or Fahrenheit for temperature?" Explain that the Fahrenheit system is still used in the U.S., although the Celsius system is used for scientific purposes.

1

■ Books open. First point to various points on the thermometer (both Fahrenheit and Celsius) and ask: "What's the temperature?" Students respond chorally (e.g., "70 degrees Fahrenheit"). Point to some temperatures below zero as well.

■ Model the task by finding 32 degrees Fahrenheit on the thermometer and asking: "What is 32 degrees Fahrenheit?" Elicit student response: "It's 0 degrees Celsius." (*Note:* On the Fahrenheit side of the thermometer, each line represents 2 degrees. On the Celsius side, each line represents 1 degree.)

■ Pairs take turns asking and answering questions about the temperatures as they do the task.

■ Check answers around the class.

Answers

a) ninety F = thirty-two degrees C
b) one hundred four F = forty C
c) seventy-two F = twenty-two C
d) three F = sixteen below zero C
e) fifty F = ten C
f) eighty-six F = thirty C
g) sixty-six F = nineteen C

2 Pair work

■ As a class, look at the sample dialogue and the chart. These are the temperatures for these cities on February 1. Ask: "What is the temperature in Quebec City?" Students answer: "It's 3 degrees Fahrenheit" or "It's 16 degrees below 0 Celsius."

■ Pairs take turns asking and answering questions about temperatures in the cities.

■ For further practice as a class, use the chart and ask: "Where is the temperature 64 degrees Fahrenheit?" Students answer: "Taipei." Continue with similar questions.

Extra practice

■ If possible, bring in a similar chart from a current English newspaper. Students work in pairs to ask and answer questions, as in part 2.

8 WHAT'S THE WEATHER LIKE? 🔈

SB p. 26 This exercise presents the seasons of the year and some additional expressions for talking about the weather.

■ Books open. Play the tape or model the sentences. Students listen and read.

■ Play the tape again; students repeat.

■ Ask questions about each picture; individual students answer. For example: "What's the weather like in picture 1? What's the temperature in picture 2? What's the season in picture 3?" Continue like this until students feel comfortable with the expressions.

■ You may want to discuss the difference between "cold" and "cool," as well as "warm" and "hot," by writing ranges of temperatures for these terms on the board.

9 LISTENING 🔈

SB p. 26 In this activity, students listen for details in a weather report.

■ Books open. Read the chart as a class. Explain that students will hear a weather report about these cities.

■ The first time, play the tape as students listen only. The second time students listen and complete the information for temperature only. The third time students listen for the conditions. The fourth time they check their answers.

■ After students compare answers with a partner, check answers as a class. If students had trouble with the answers, play the tape a final time so they hear the correct information.

Tape transcript

Listen to the weather reports for the cities below. Write the temperature and check off the weather conditions.

REPORTER: Now let's look at the weather in different cities around the world. In Sapporo, Japan, they're having a very cold winter. Today it's twenty below zero Celsius. Now that's cold. And it's snowing. That's right, it's snowing in Sapporo.

The weather in Bangkok, Thailand, is very different. It's really warm and sunny there. It's twenty-eight degrees Celsius. A beautiful day in Bangkok.

Over in the United States, in Miami, the weather is not as nice. It's only twenty degrees Celsius. So it's very cool in Miami, and it's cloudy.

Now, what about in South America? They're having a hot summer there. In Rio de Janeiro, it's very hot – it's thirty-five degrees Celsius. *And* it's raining. Not a nice day.

In Buenos Aires, [*fades out*].

Answers

a) *Sapporo:* 20 degrees below 0 C / cold, snowing
b) *Bangkok:* 28 degrees C / warm, sunny
c) *Miami:* 20 degrees C / cool, cloudy
d) *Rio de Janeiro:* 35 degrees C / hot, raining

10 **CLOTHES AND WEATHER**

`SB p. 27` This activity reviews the present continuous tense and vocabulary about weather and clothes.

1 Pair work

■ Books open. Look at the pictures and model sentences as a class.

■ Students work individually and write three sentences about each picture.

■ Students join with a partner to compare sentences and help each other. Circulate and provide help as needed.

■ Bring the class back together. Each student reads one sentence to the class, and the class guesses which picture it is about.

2 Pair work

■ In pairs, students talk about today's weather and what they are wearing.

■ Ask a few pairs to share their answers with the class.

INTERCHANGE 4:
What's the weather like?

`SB p. IC-5` This activity reviews the themes and grammar points of the unit.

1 Pair work

■ Books open to page IC-5. Explain that this is a weather map. Ask a few questions based on the chart, such as: "Where is it very cold? Where is it sunny?"

■ Students work in pairs to answer the five questions.

■ Check answers around the class. Answers will vary depending on how you define "warm" and "very hot." (*Note:* In the sample answers below, "warm" is considered 70–84 degrees F, or 21–29 C, and "very hot" 85 degrees F, or 30 C, and above.)

Sample answers

a) *sunny and warm:* Los Angeles, Honolulu, Bogotá, Buenos Aires, Lima, Caracas

b) *snowing:* Anchorage, Winnipeg, Chicago, Quebec City, Montreal, Boston

c) *raining:* Vancouver, São Paulo, Miami, Washington, D.C.

d) *very hot:* Santiago, São Paulo

e) *below freezing:* Anchorage, Winnipeg, Chicago, Quebec City, Montreal, Boston, New York

2 Pair work

■ Pairs take turns asking and answering questions about the weather map.

■ Bring the class back together and have several students ask one of their questions to the class.

Review of Units 1–4

This unit reviews prepositions of place, conjunctions, imperatives, the present continuous, and the vocabulary of the first four units.

UNIT PLAN

1 Prepositions of Place: *Reviews* this/these, my/your, *questions with* where, *and the vocabulary of common objects*

2 Listening: *Reviews the vocabulary of clothes and furniture, and prepositions of place*

3 Same or Different?: *Reviews the present continuous, conjunctions, and clothes*

4 Instructions: *Reviews verbs and imperatives*

5 What's the Question?: *Reviews the functions and question words of the first four units*

6 What's Strange About This Picture?: *Reviews the present continuous, conjunctions, and the vocabulary of the first four units*

1 PREPOSITIONS OF PLACE

`SB p. 28` This exercise reviews *this/these*, questions with *where, my/your*, prepositions of place, and the vocabulary of common objects.

Group work

■ Students read the instructions and the model sentences. Go over them as a class.

■ Demonstrate the task by acting it out with a student. Ask the student to identify two items he or she is carrying (e.g., "This is my pen. This is my book."). Take the items from the student and say: "Close your eyes." Hide the items. Tell the student: "Open your eyes." The student asks about the items, like this: "Where is my pen?" You answer: "It's under the desk."

■ Students do the task in small groups. Circulate to make sure that all students in the group have a chance to participate.

2 | LISTENING 🔲

SB p. 28 This exercise reviews listening for prepositions of place, articles of clothing, and furniture.

■ Use the instructions and picture to set the context: Tim and his mother are looking for Tim's things in his room. Where are they?

■ Elicit the name of each item pictured (a–e).

■ Play the tape as students listen only.

■ Play the tape again; students do the task. Play the tape two or three more times, as necessary.

■ Students check their answers in pairs, and then as a class.

■ Play the tape a final time if students have questions about answers.

Tape transcript

Tim is looking for things in his room. His mother is helping him. Listen and mark the location of each item in the picture.

TIM: Mom, where are my running shoes?
MOM: I think they're under your bed.
TIM: Oh, right. And what about my blue jeans?
MOM: They're here, behind the chair.
TIM: Oh, good. Hm. But where is my hat, then?
MOM: Your hat is over *there*, in front of the desk.
TIM: Great. Oh – and my watch. Where's my watch?
MOM: It's *on* the desk. Wait a minute, Tim. You aren't wearing your glasses.
TIM: OK. Right, my glasses. Where are they?
MOM: They're next to the bed, right in front of you. Tim, no! [*sound of crunching glass as Tim steps on his glasses*]
TIM: You're right. They're next to the bed. On the floor.

Answers

(Answers appear in this order in the picture, starting at the top and reading down and left to right.)

d
c
a, e, b

3 | SAME OR DIFFERENT?

SB p. 28 This exercise reviews the present continuous, the vocabulary of clothes, and the conjunctions *and* and *but*.

Pair work

■ Go over the instructions and the model sentences with the class. Demonstrate further by writing the headings "Same" and "Different" on the board and calling on volunteers to compare two students by offering a sentence in each category.

■ Students choose two classmates and write five sentences comparing what is the same and different about their clothes. Circulate to provide help as needed.

■ Students check each other's work in pairs.

■ Circulate and check students' work. Then share answers as a class.

4 | INSTRUCTIONS

SB p. 29 This exercise reviews imperatives.

Pair work

■ Explain the task. Students write their own instructions using the words in their book.

■ Students work individually.

■ When they have finished, students work in pairs. They take turns saying and following each other's instructions.

■ If you wish, ask for volunteers to perform their instructions for the class, or ask a student to read his or her instructions while the class performs them.

5 WHAT'S THE QUESTION?

SB p. 29 This exercise reviews functions and the question words of the first four units.

1

■ Explain the task: Students match the questions with the answers.

■ Students do the task individually.

■ When they have finished, check answers as a class.

■ Pairs practice asking and answering the questions.

Answers

a) 6	f) 10
b) 8	g) 3
c) 1	h) 4
d) 9	i) 7
e) 5	j) 2

2 Pair work

■ Students work in pairs. They take turns asking and answering the questions in part 1 with their own information.

■ If you wish, bring the class back together and ask the questions to different students.

6 WHAT'S STRANGE ABOUT THIS PICTURE?

SB p. 29 This exercise reviews the present continuous, conjunctions, and the vocabulary of the first four units.

Pair work

■ Look at the picture as a class. Students look for things that are strange. Demonstrate the task by saying the model sentence. (*Note:* It is also correct to say: "A woman is swimming, but she's wearing a blouse and a hat.") Ask for a volunteer to find another strange thing.

■ Students write the sentences individually. (*Note:* There are more than five strange things in the picture.) Circulate to provide help.

■ Students share their answers in pairs, and then as a class.

Sample answers

– It's warm and sunny, but a man is wearing a coat, a hat, gloves, and boots.
– A woman is playing tennis, but she's wearing a suit and high heels.
– A man is playing tennis with an umbrella, and he's wearing a suit and a tie.
– A boy is wearing pajamas.
– A man is wearing one blue shoe and one white shoe.
– A man is standing in the water, but he's wearing a shoe (and sock), and he's carrying a briefcase.

5 What are you doing?

This unit has two cycles and presents expressions for talking about the time and daily activities. It introduces present continuous questions with *what + doing* and present continuous yes/no questions, and it emphasizes yes/no question intonation.

UNIT PLAN

Cycle 1

1 Conversation: *Introduces time expressions and present continuous questions with* what + doing

2 What Time Is It? (1): *A practice activity for telling the time*

3 Grammar Focus: *Presents present continuous questions with* what + doing

4 Listening: *Practices listening for time expressions*

Interchange 5: *A fluency activity that practices time expressions and the present continuous*

5 Snapshot: *Introduces vocabulary for watches and clocks*

6 What Time Is It? (2): *Extends vocabulary for telling the time*

WORKBOOK: Exercises 1–4 on pages 17 to 19

Cycle 2

7 Conversation: *Introduces yes/no questions in the present continuous*

8 Pronunciation: *Practices intonation in statements and yes/no questions*

9 Listening: *Uses nonverbal listening cues to practice the present continuous*

10 Grammar Focus: *Practices present continuous questions and statements*

11 Reading: *Practices reading for the main idea and using inference skills*

WORKBOOK: Exercises 5–6 on pages 19 and 20

[1] CONVERSATION

SB p. 30 This conversation introduces present continuous questions with *what + doing* and expressions for asking and talking about the time.

■ Students cover the text and look at the pictures of Deborah and John. Ask students what they are wearing.

■ Books closed. On the board write: "Where is John? Where is Deborah?" Play the tape; students listen in order to answer the questions. Then ask the questions again. (Answers: John is in Sydney, Australia. Deborah is in Los Angeles, in the U.S.)

■ Books open. Play the tape again. Students read and listen.

■ Present the conversation line by line; students repeat. Try to elicit the meanings of "attending" and "conference."

■ Students practice the dialogue in pairs using the Look Up and Say technique.

■ If you wish, have a few pairs act out their conversation for the class.

[2] WHAT TIME IS IT? (1)

SB p. 30 This exercise presents expressions for giving the time and the parts of the day.

1

■ Play the tape or model the sentences. Students read and listen.

■ Play the tape again. This time students repeat each sentence.

■ Point to one of the pictures and ask the class: "What time is it?" Students answer chorally and then individually. Continue until students feel comfortable with the expressions.

2

■ Students work in pairs to say the times another way. (*Note:* People generally say "in the morning" from 1:00 A.M. until noon, "in the afternoon" from noon until around 6:00 P.M., "in the evening" from 6:00 P.M. until 10:00 or 11:00 P.M., and "at night" from 7:00 or 8:00 P.M. until just before 1:00 A.M.)

Answers

b) It's midnight. *or* It's 12:00 midnight.
c) It's 3:00 P.M.
d) It's three o'clock in the morning.
e) It's nine o'clock in the morning.
f) It's four o'clock in the afternoon.

Extra practice

1. Draw a clock on the board or bring in a clock with movable hands. Set the hands to various times, and ask what time it is. (5 minutes)

2. Students working alone draw five clocks on a piece of paper. Each clock should show a different time. Students label each clock "morning," "afternoon," or "evening" and then join with a partner and take turns asking and answering about the time on each other's clocks. (5 minutes)

[3] GRAMMAR FOCUS: Present continuous: *what + doing*

SB p. 31 Here, students practice the present continuous tense with *what + doing* questions.

1

■ Books open. Point out the headings for each picture, which give the city and time. Then play the tape or model the sentences under each picture. Students read and listen.

■ Play the tape again; students repeat. For the last picture, students say what they themselves are doing now.

2 Pair work

■ Students work in pairs and take turns asking and answering the questions. Help students with the meaning of "who."

■ Bring the class back together, and call on individual students to answer the questions.

Extra practice

■ Have students work individually to write three more questions about the pictures. Then lead a chain drill: Student A asks Student B a question; B answers and asks Student C a question, and so on around the class.

4 LISTENING 📼

SB p. 32 This activity practices listening for the time.

■ Books open. Explain the task: Students listen to a conversation between Sue and Tom, who are calling their friends in different cities. Students listen for the time in the cities.

■ Play the tape once while students listen only. Then play the tape two or three times more as students write down the time in each city.

■ Have students compare answers in pairs. Then play the tape again while students check their answers.

■ Go over the answers with the class.

Tape transcript

It's seven P.M. in New York. Sue and Tom are calling their friends in different cities. What time is it in Bangkok? Tokyo? Brasília?   -

SUE: What time is it now?
TOM: It's seven o'clock.
SUE: Good. If it's seven P.M. in New York, then it's seven A.M. in Bangkok. So I'm calling Permsak right now. [*picks up phone*]
TOM: Permsak? If it's seven A.M., Permsak is sleeping.
SUE: [*hangs up phone*] You're right.
TOM: Wait a minute, what time is it in Tokyo?
SUE: It's nine A.M.
TOM: Great. [*picks up phone and dials*]
SUE: So, what are you doing?
TOM: I'm calling Kyoko in Tokyo. She's awake.
SUE: But Kyoko is in Brasília this week. Remember?
TOM: Oh, right. [*hangs up phone*]
SUE: Here's her telephone number at the hotel.
TOM: So what time is it in Brasília?
SUE: It's nine o'clock in the evening. Hm. Kyoko is probably watching television right now. [*picks up phone and dials*]
TOM: So, are you calling Kyoko?
SUE: Yes, I am.
TOM: Great. We have to tell someone about our new baby . . . [*infant cries in the background*]

Answers

Bangkok: 7:00 A.M.
Tokyo: 9:00 A.M.
Brasília: 9:00 P.M.

Extra practice

■ Play the tape again. Ask: "What are Permsak and Kyoko probably doing?" Students listen for the answers. (Answers: Permsak is probably sleeping. Kyoko is probably watching TV.)

INTERCHANGE 5: Time zones

SB p. IC-8 This activity practices time expressions and the present continuous.

■ Books open to page IC-8. Go over the map as a class. Point out the times at the bottom. Check comprehension by asking: "What time is it in Santiago?" (It's 7:00 A.M. / It's seven o'clock in the morning.) "What are people doing?" (They're getting up.)

Pair work

■ Students work in pairs and take turns asking and answering questions about what time it is in the different cities and what people are doing there. They can use the expressions in the box for their answers, or they can use their own expressions. (Students may not know the expressions "getting dressed" and "shopping." You can use the illustrations on page 34 of the Student's Book to explain them, if you wish.)

■ When things begin to quiet down, bring the class back together, and ask selected pairs to tell the class about some of the different cities.

Extra practice

■ As a class, calculate the actual time in the cities listed and add one or two others if you like. Students change partners to do the activity again, this time using the actual time to ask and answer the questions. (5 minutes)

5 SNAPSHOT

SB p. 32 This activity presents vocabulary for different kinds of clocks and watches.

■ Books closed. Students mingle around the room and count the number of different kinds of watches and clocks they can find.

■ Ask students how many different kinds they found.

■ Books open. Lead students through the Snapshot. Ask them to write a check mark next to the kinds of watches and clocks they found in the class.

■ Students work individually to answer the questions. Then students share their answers in pairs or small groups.

■ As a class, make a list on the board of the kinds of watches and clocks people have. What kind is most popular? Least popular?

6 WHAT TIME IS IT? (2)

SB p. 32 This activity presents expressions for giving more exact time before or after the hour.

Note: There are many ways of saying the time in English, and your students may hear these variants:

a quarter to three = a quarter of three
twenty to eight = twenty before eight,
                          twenty of eight
nine thirty = half past nine
nine twenty = twenty past nine

It is not necessary to present these forms at this point unless students ask about them.

1

■ Books open. Play the tape or model the times. Students read and repeat.

■ Write these times on the board: 4:20, 6:55, 2:05, 3:30, 11:40. Lead choral and individual repetition of the times. Use both ways of saying the time when appropriate. If you wish, interrupt your practice every so often and ask: "What time is it now?"

2   Pair work

■ Pairs take turns asking and answering about the time shown on the six clocks.

■ Check answers as a class.

Answers

It's twenty after two (2:20).
It's ten to seven (6:50).
It's a quarter to nine (8:45).
It's five after eleven (eleven-oh-five).
It's a quarter after three (3:15).
It's four thirty.

Extra practice

■ Students work alone to draw five clocks similar to those in part 2.

■ Students ask and answer questions about each other's clocks.

7 CONVERSATION

SB p. 33 This conversation introduces yes/no questions in the present continuous tense.

■ Books open. Set the scene by asking students questions about the picture of Mr. and Mrs. Ford. For example: "What is Mrs. Ford doing? What time is it? Where is Mr. Ford? What is he doing?"

■ Play the tape. Students listen and read.

■ Present the conversation line by line. Elicit the meanings of the following expressions by having students look at the surrounding language and guess the meaning from context:

"Hey!" (used to get someone's attention)
"I'm staying in bed." = "I'm not getting up."
"If I'm awake." = "If I'm not sleeping."

■ Students practice the conversation in pairs. Encourage them to use the Look Up and Say technique.

■ If you wish, have a few pairs act out the conversation for the class.

8 PRONUNCIATION 🔲

SB p. 33 This activity practices the intonation of statements and yes/no questions.

1

- Books open. Explain "intonation": It is the musical pitch of the voice. Demonstrate by humming. Then say the two sentences "I'm getting up now." and "Are you getting up?" After you say each sentence, hum it so that students hear the change in pitch.

- Explain that intonation carries important meaning in English. In this exercise, intonation helps listeners to tell the difference between a question and a statement.

> **Rule**
>
> Questions with an answer of "yes" or "no" always end with rising intonation. Statements end with falling intonation.

- Play the tape or model the sentences as students listen and read.

- Lead students in choral and individual practice of the four sentences. Then students practice in pairs.

2

- Explain the task: Students listen to single sentences on the tape. They listen for the intonation at the end of the sentence and then say whether the sentence is a yes/no question or a statement.

- Play the tape as many times as necessary as students do the task individually.

- Have students compare answers with a partner; then go over the answers with the class.

- Play the tape a final time so that students can check their work.

Tape transcript

a) Is this your umbrella?
b) Our telephone number is 555-3291.
c) I'm from South America.
d) Is it cold in Miami today?
e) This is an eyeglass case.
f) Are they wearing warm clothes?

Answers

a) Q   b) S   c) S   d) Q   e) S   f) Q

---

9 LISTENING: Saturday chores 🔲

SB p. 33 This activity uses sound effects to teach some new expressions.

- Books open. Illustrate the word "chores" by pointing to the pictures. Go over the pronunciation of each expression.

- Explain the task: Students listen to the sounds of people doing chores. They do not hear any language. They write the picture number next to the correct description.

- Play the tape several times. Then ask after each sound: "What is the person doing?" Students answer "shopping," "vacuuming," etc.

- Students compare their answers with a partner, or review them as a class.

Answers

a) 4   b) 3   c) 1   d) 2

10 GRAMMAR FOCUS:
Present continuous: yes/no
questions 🔲

SB p. 34 This activity practices the present
continuous tense with yes/no questions and short
answers.

Grammar note

In this activity students form their own
questions. Yes/no questions are formed from a
statement by inverting the subject and the *be*
verb. If you wish, show how this is done by
writing the following sentences on the board.
Use arrows to show that the subject and verb
change places:

He is having breakfast.

Is he having breakfast?

In addition, you may want to review the
spelling rules for present continuous verbs
(see Unit 4, ex. 5, p. 23 of the Student's
Book). Point out that short answers for the
present continuous are the same as for the
verb *be* (see Unit 3, ex. 9, p. 19 of the
Student's Book).

■ Books open. Play the tape or model the
sentences in the box. Students listen, read, and
repeat.

■ Lead choral and individual repetition of the
model sentences. Pay attention to intonation and
stress.

1 Pair work

■ Look at the first picture as a class. Ask the class
questions about the picture, using the sample
dialogue as a model. The class can answer
chorally, or students can answer individually.

■ In pairs, students take turns asking and
answering questions about the Fords' activities
during the day. Circulate and give help as needed.

■ If you wish, pairs can describe one of the
pictures to the rest of the class.

2 Pair work

■ Students work individually to write five more
questions about the Fords, using the sentence in
the Student's Book as a model.

■ Students ask and answer each other's questions
in pairs.

Optional activity: *Diary*

■ As a homework activity, ask students to keep a
diary of one day in their lives. Explain that a
diary is a notebook; people write their actions and
thoughts in it.

■ Tell students to keep a diary of what they are
doing throughout the day, like this:

It's 8:00 A.M. I'm getting up.
It's 8:15. I'm having breakfast. (etc.)

■ Students bring their diaries to class and share
their activities with a partner or with the class.

11 READING 🔘

SB p. 35 Part 1 of this exercise practices reading for the main idea; part 2 practices inference skills.

1

■ Books open. Students look at the four photos. Ask the class what the people are doing in each of the pictures.

■ Students read the four paragraphs and match them to the appropriate pictures. Tell students to read for the main idea, and not to worry about words they do not know. (*Note:* The names of the people – Chris, Terry, Stacy, and Pat – can be either men's or women's names in English. Therefore the names do not give the answers away.)

■ Tell students to circle the key words that helped them find the answer.

■ Have students compare answers and key words with a partner; then go over them as a class.

■ If you wish, after students have done the task, play the tape so that students can listen as they read the paragraphs. Do not play the tape *before* students do the task, because the sex of the speakers will give away one of the answers.

■ If you wish, ask students to underline words they do not know in the paragraphs. Encourage students to guess the meaning from the context of the paragraph or from the photo that accompanies the paragraph.

Answers

a) 2　　b) 4　　c) 3　　d) 1

2

■ Students can do this inferencing activity individually or in pairs. First, students read the four sentences and find the right paragraph for each sentence. Tell them to look at the key words they circled earlier. In some cases, they may help the students make the match.

■ Check answers around the class to make sure students have correctly matched the sentences to the paragraphs (see Answers below).

■ Next students decide where in the paragraph the sentence goes. If they have trouble, work on the first sentence as a class.

Answers

a) paragraph b; add it after the last sentence (*reason:* They're working hard, so they're feeling tired now.)
b) paragraph d; add it after the last sentence (*reason:* It's starting to rain, and she needs an umbrella because she's sitting outdoors.)
c) paragraph a; add it before the last sentence (*reason:* She is shopping for these things – a bathing suit, sandals, sunglasses. This makes a list.)
d) paragraph c; add it after sentence 1 (*reason:* They're driving around, looking at people, *and* listening to the radio. These activities aren't "anything special.")

3 Group work

■ Break the class into groups of four to six. Ask students to imagine that today is Saturday. They decide as a group what they are doing, then write five sentences about it.

■ Bring the class back together; groups take turns reporting to the class "what they are doing" (in their imagination). The group can mime the activities as they describe them.

■ If you wish, have the class vote on which group is doing the most interesting things.

6 How do you go to work?

This unit has two cycles and introduces present tense statements and questions to talk about the themes of transportation, family, and daily schedules. Both regular and irregular verbs are covered.

UNIT PLAN

Cycle 1

1 Snapshot: *Introduces vocabulary for transportation*

2 Conversation: *Illustrates the difference between present continuous and simple present*

3 Word Power: *Builds vocabulary for talking about family members*

4 Listening: *Introduces the present tense and practices listening for details about family members*

5 Grammar Focus: *Practices present tense statements with regular and irregular verbs*

6 Spelling and Pronunciation: *Practices third person singular* s

WORKBOOK: Exercises 1–3 on pages 21 and 22

Cycle 2

7 Conversation: *Introduces present tense questions and expressions for discussing personal schedules*

8 Grammar Focus: *Practices present tense questions and present time expressions*

Interchange 6: *A class survey about people's lives that reviews present tense questions and statements*

9 Days of the Week: *A fluency practice activity*

10 Reading: *Reading about people's work schedules for detail*

WORKBOOK: Exercises 4–7 on pages 23 and 24

1   SNAPSHOT

SB p. 36 This activity introduces the topic of transportation.

■ Books closed. Tell students how you get to class and how other people travel to work in your city. Mention all types of transportation available.

■ Make a chart on the board.

TRANSPORTATION	
Public	Private
bus	car

Ask students to name forms of private and public transportation. (Additional forms of private transportation might include bicycle, motorcycle, and scooter.)

■ Ask students which form of transportation they think is most popular in the United States. Record their answers on the board.

■ Books open. Students read the Snapshot individually and compare the information with that on the board. Explain that "commute" = travel to work.

■ Read the two questions with the class. Then have students write the answers individually.

■ Students compare their answers in pairs or small groups. Ask several students to share their responses with the class.

2   CONVERSATION

SB p. 36 This conversation introduces present tense statements and questions, as well as expressions for talking about home, commuting, and family. It also contrasts the present and present continuous tenses.

■ Books open. Students cover the text with a piece of paper. Set the scene by looking at the picture of Charles and Julia as a class. Ask: "What are Charles and Julia talking about?"

■ Books closed. On the board write:

> What is Charles's problem?
> How does Julia go to work?

■ Play the tape; students listen in order to answer these questions. (Answers: Charles's car isn't working. Julia walks to work.)

■ Books open. Play the tape again; students read and listen.

■ Present the conversation line by line. Explain that "What's the matter?" = "What's the problem?" Illustrate the meaning of "tow truck," "suburbs," and "downtown" with simple drawings on the board. "Suburbs" and "downtown" can be illustrated like this:

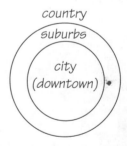

■ Students practice the conversation in pairs. Encourage them to use the Look Up and Say technique and to try to speak with the same intonation as the actors on the tape.

■ If you wish, have several pairs act out their conversation for the class.

3 WORD POWER: Family relationships 🔲

SB p. 37 This activity presents vocabulary about the family.

■ Books open. Model the words in the picture; students read and repeat.

■ Students complete the sentences individually. Go over the example, and if necessary, do sentence (b) as a class to get students started.

■ Students compare their answers with a partner or around the class. Then play the tape (or model the answers) so that students can check their work.

■ If you wish, play the tape again and have students repeat the sentences.

Tape transcript with answers

a) Anne is Charles's <u>wife</u>.
b) Jason and Sophia are his <u>children</u>.
c) Charles is Anne's <u>husband</u>.
d) Jason is Anne's <u>son</u>.
e) Sophia is Anne's <u>daughter</u>.
f) Jason is Sophia's <u>brother</u>.
g) Sophia is Jason's <u>sister</u>.
h) Charles and Anne are Jason's <u>parents</u>.

4 LISTENING 🔲

SB p. 37 This activity practices listening comprehension of present tense statements about people's lives.

1

■ Books open. Students cover the text with a piece of paper. Show the class the three pictures and say, "This is Charles's family." Ask: "Who are the people in the pictures? Where do they live: in the suburbs, the city, or the country?" Students look at each picture and guess.

■ Play the tape as students listen and read.

■ Play the tape again; students listen and repeat the sentences. Lead choral and individual repetition if you wish, until students are comfortable with the language.

2 Pair work

■ Explain the task: Students listen to members of Charles's family talk about their lives. Students write down who is talking, based on the information in part 1.

■ Play the tape in segments, pausing after each monologue. Students work in pairs to decide who is talking. To encourage partners to communicate, write on the board:

It's his _____ because _____ .

Play each segment several times.

■ If you wish, encourage students to write down two key words as they listen. This will help them find the answer.

■ When you have finished playing the tape, compare answers as a class. Then play the tape a final time so that students can compare the monologues to the correct answers.

Tape transcript for part 2

2 *Pair work* Listen to people in Charles's family talking. Who are they?

a) I live with my mom and dad in the suburbs. I go to school every day with my brother. We take the bus to school.

b) My husband and I live in a big house in the country. My husband still drives his car to work every day, but I stay at home. I'm retired.

c) I live downtown in an apartment. I live alone. I don't need a car because I walk to work.

d) My husband and I live in a nice house in the suburbs. We have a son and a daughter, and we have two cars. I drive my car to work every day.

Answers

a) <u>3</u> his daughter, Sofia
b) <u>2</u> his mother
c) <u>4</u> his sister
d) <u>1</u> his wife, Anne

~~MAR~~ FOCUS:
~~...~~ense statements

◄ This activity practices simple present ~~..~~se statements with regular and irregular verbs.

> **Grammar notes**
>
> 1. The simple present tense is used to talk about things that happen every day (e.g., "We both go to work by car") or that are true in general (e.g., "I have a car").
>
> 2. *Don't* and *doesn't* are the contractions of the full forms *do not* and *does not*, which are more formal.

■ Books open. Play the tape or model the language in the box. Students listen and repeat. Point out to students that "don't" = "do not" and "doesn't" = "does not."

■ Apply the language to yourself and the class. Begin by saying: "I live in the city. I don't live in the country." Then have students make similar statements about themselves.

1

■ Explain the task: Students choose which verb is the correct form.

■ Students do the task individually.

■ Have students compare their answers with a partner. Then play the tape while students check and revise their work.

■ Go over the answers with the class.

■ If you wish, play the tape again or model the statements and have students practice.

Tape transcript with answers

a) I <u>live</u> with my parents.
b) We <u>live</u> downtown.
c) My parents <u>have</u> an apartment.
d) I <u>walk</u> to work.
e) I <u>don't</u> need a car.
f) My mother <u>doesn't</u> walk to work.

g) She <u>uses</u> public transportation.
h) She <u>takes</u> the subway.
i) My father is retired, so he <u>doesn't</u> have a job.
j) But he <u>does</u> a lot of work at home.
k) He also <u>watches</u> television.
l) I <u>have</u> a brother and a sister.
m) My sister <u>has</u> a husband and three children.
n) They <u>live</u> in a house in the country.
o) The children <u>go</u> to school by bus.
p) My brother <u>has</u> an apartment in the city.
q) He <u>lives</u> alone.
r) He <u>doesn't</u> have a car.
s) He <u>uses</u> public transportation.
t) He <u>goes</u> to work by bus.

2 Pair work

■ Students work alone to write five sentences about their family, similar to those in part 1.

■ Circulate to help with vocabulary and check for accuracy.

■ Students compare their sentences with a partner. Pairs can either exchange papers or take turns reading their statements to each other.

3 Class activity

■ Students use the five sentences they wrote for part 2 and tell the class how their partner is the same or different. Pairs present their information to the class.

■ In large classes, you may want to conduct this activity in groups of eight to ten.

Extra practice

■ In order to contrast the present continuous and simple present tenses, ask students to look again at the conversation in exercise 2 on page 36. Tell them to find three sentences that give information about "right now" and four sentences that tell about things that happen "every day."

■ Students compare answers in pairs before checking answers as a class.

Answers

Sentences about "right now" (present continuous)
1. My car isn't working.
2. I'm waiting for a tow truck.
3. Yes, my wife is coming to get me.

Sentences about "every day" (simple present)
1. Do you live near here?
2. No, we live in the suburbs.
3. I live downtown, with my parents.
4. I walk to work.

Optional activity: *Who am I?*

■ Collect all the papers from part 2, on which students wrote five sentences about themselves. Mix them up and hand them back to different students. Call on students to read the paper they have; the other students try to guess who wrote the paper.

6 SPELLING AND PRONUNCIATION: Third person singular *s* 🔲

SB p. 39 This activity practices the spelling and pronunciation of verbs in the third person singular of the simple present tense.

Note: The pronunciation of *s* in the third person singular follows the same rules as the pronunciation of *s* in plural nouns (see page 22, Unit 2, ex. 2, of this Teacher's Manual).

1

■ Books open. Play the tape or model the words. Students listen and read.

■ Play the tape or model the words again; students repeat chorally and then individually.

■ If students are having trouble producing or distinguishing /s/ and /z/, tell them to put their fingers over their throat as they practice the two sounds so that they can feel the difference between the voiceless /s/ and the voiced /z/.

2 Pair work

■ Students do the task in pairs, changing roles so that they each read from list B.

■ Bring the class back together, and ask students around the class to say a verb from list B.

Extra practice

■ On the board write:

1	2	3	4
s = /s/	s = /z/	s = /ɪz/	irregular

■ Read any pair of verbs from the exercise. Ask students to tell you if it belongs in list 1, 2, 3, or 4. List each verb under the appropriate column.

■ Check answers around the class.

Answers

1 s = /s/	2 s = /z/	3 s = /ɪz/	4 irregular
walks	wears	closes	says
works	plays	erases	does
writes	runs		
	goes		
	swims		
	snows		
	rains		
	opens		

7 CONVERSATION 🔲

SB p. 39 This conversation introduces present tense questions about daily activities.

■ Books open. Students cover the text with a piece of paper. Set the scene by looking at the picture of Matthew and Amy. Ask: "Where are Matthew and Amy? What are they talking about?"

■ Books closed. On the board write: What time does Matthew get up on Sundays?

■ Play the tape; students listen for the answer. Ask the class to answer as a group. (Answer: noon)

(instructions continue on next page)

1

■ Books open. Play the tape again; students listen and read.

■ Present the conversation line by line; students repeat. Explain that "on Sundays" = "every Sunday" and that "sleep in" = "sleep late" or "get up late."

■ Students practice the conversation in pairs using the Look Up and Say technique.

■ If you wish, have several pairs act out the conversation for the class.

2

■ Explain the task: Students listen to the rest of Matthew and Amy's conversation and answer the two questions.

■ Play the rest of the conversation two or three times.

■ Students compare their answers with a partner and then with the class.

Tape transcript for part 2

2 Listen to the rest of the conversation. a) What time does Amy get up on weekdays? b) What time does Matthew get up on weekdays?

MATTHEW: OK. So, let's have breakfast at one o'clock, then go to the park, and then go to a movie.
AMY: A movie? OK – if it's an early movie. Remember that I get up early on weekdays.
MATTHEW: So what time do you get up, exactly?
AMY: At six A.M.
MATTHEW: Six A.M.? Wow, that *is* early.
AMY: Yeah, well, I leave for work at seven in the morning. What about you?
MATTHEW: Well, I work from noon until eight o'clock at night. So I get up at ten.
AMY: Lucky you!

Answers

a) 6:00 A.M.   b) 10:00 A.M.

8 GRAMMAR FOCUS:
Present tense questions

SB p. 40 This activity presents present tense questions with *do*: yes/no questions and wh-questions. It also introduces more time expressions.

> **Grammar notes**
>
> 1. Present tense questions use the auxiliary word *do*. It may be helpful to give students this formula for yes/no questions:
>
> **Do** I/you/we/they (verb) . . . ?
> **Does** he/she/it (verb) . . . ?
>
> 2. For wh-questions, you use the same formula, except you place the wh-word at the beginning:
>
> What **do** I/you/we/they (verb) . . . ?
> What **does** he/she/it (verb) . . . ?

■ Books open. Play the tape or model the sentences in the grammar focus box. Students listen and read.

■ Play the tape or model the sentences again; students repeat.

■ Present the time expressions in the box using the tape or by modeling them; students repeat.

1

■ Students work alone to unscramble the questions.

■ Students compare their work with a partner. Then check answers as a class.

■ Students practice the conversations in pairs. If you wish, have pairs perform for the class.

Answers

What time do you get up?
Does Julia live alone?
What time does the bus come?
Do you have breakfast every day?

2 Pair work

- Explain that students work individually and write answers to the questions with their own information.

- Circulate to help with vocabulary and accuracy.

- Partners take turns asking and answering the questions.

- Bring the class back together, and ask the questions to several students around the room. Alternatively, ask students to raise their hands to show, for example, how many eat breakfast every day.

INTERCHANGE 6: Class survey

SB p. IC-9 This communication activity practices asking and answering present tense questions about students' daily lives.

- Books open to page IC-9. Explain the task and model the sample conversations with a student. Explain that every student must try to find one person in the class who does each thing on the list. If someone answers yes to their question, they write down the person's name.

- If you wish, go through the items on the list and have students form questions as a class chorally before they begin the activity.

- Everyone mingles and asks each other questions. Encourage students to change interview partners every two or three questions, so that students get to talk to a variety of people.

- When things begin to quiet down, bring the class back together.

2 Class activity

- Go around the room and ask students to make a statement about a person they talked to. Tell students to use the model in the book as an example. Give everyone a chance to say at least one thing. If your class is very large, do this task in groups of eight to ten.

9 DAYS OF THE WEEK

SB p. 41 This activity presents the days of the week and practices talking about daily schedules.

1

- Books open. Play the tape or model the days of the week. Students listen and repeat.

- To practice, say a day of the week, and have the class quickly say the day that follows:

T: Tuesday.
Ss: Wednesday.
T: Thursday.
Ss: Friday.

Extra practice

- Groups of no more than seven write the days of the week on small slips of paper.

- Groups place these slips of paper where everyone in the group can easily reach them.

- Designate a leader in each group. Then call out a day of the week. The group leader quickly finds the slip of paper with the *next* day of the week written on it and says this day. Moving to the left, the student does the same with the day that follows. Students continue around the group until they have picked up all the slips and said all the days of the week. The group that finishes first is the winner of this round.

- Play several times. The group that wins the most rounds is class champion. (10 minutes)

2 Pair work

- Model one or two of the questions and answers for the class.

- In pairs, students take turns asking and answering the questions.

- Bring the class back together, and have individual students choose questions to ask of other students in the class.

10 READING 🔲

SB p. 41 This activity practices reading for detail and reading to compare information.

1

■ Before doing the task, define the word "regular," if necessary (used in the middle paragraph). "Regular" = always the same, it doesn't change.

■ Explain that there is one wrong word in each paragraph. Students should find the word and correct it.

■ Students read to find the mistake.

■ Students compare their choices with a partner and read again if they disagree on the answers.

■ Go over the answers with the class. If you wish, play the tape, which gives the correct word in each paragraph.

Answers

Randall Kelly: (last sentence) . . . I only work on ~~weekends~~ weekdays.

Andrea Morris: (next to last sentence) My job is interesting, but my schedule is ~~regular~~ irregular. (*Note:* You may also accept ". . . my schedule ~~is~~ isn't regular.")

Rob Jefferson: (next to last sentence) I go to bed at five in the morning and sleep until two in the ~~morning~~ afternoon.

2

■ Read the questions with the class. Then have students silently read the descriptions again and answer the questions. If you wish, play the tape as they read. [*Note:* If students cannot find something they like about someone's schedule for question (d), they can write something they do not like.]

■ Students compare answers in pairs and then as a class. Ask students to share their answer to the last question with the class.

Answers

a) Randall Kelly gets up early. Sometimes Andrea Morris gets up early. Rob Jefferson gets up late.
b) Rob Jefferson works at night. Randall Kelly works during the day. Sometimes Andrea Morris works at night, and sometimes she works during the day.
c) Rob Jefferson and Andrea Morris work on weekends. Randall Kelly and Andrea Morris work on weekdays.
d) Answers will vary. Sample answer: Randall Kelly goes to bed at nine. I like that. I go to bed early, too.

3

■ Students work alone to write five sentences about their own schedule.

■ Circulate to provide help and check for accuracy.

■ In small groups, students take turns reading their sentences.

■ Have groups decide who has the best and the worst schedule, and share them with the class.

7 Does the apartment have a view?

This unit has two cycles and introduces expressions for talking about housing and home furnishings. It focuses on present tense questions with short answers and *there is/there are*.

UNIT PLAN

Cycle 1

1 Snapshot: *Introduces vocabulary for the rooms of a house*

2 Conversation: *Introduces present tense yes/no questions and short answers*

3 Grammar Focus: *Fluency practice for present tense yes/no questions*

4 Listening: *Practices listening for the gist of descriptions of people's homes*

5 Dream House: *A writing and pair work exercise that reviews the vocabulary and grammar of this cycle*

WORKBOOK: Exercises 1–3 on pages 25 and 26

Cycle 2

6 Conversation: *Introduces* there is *and* there are

7 Word Power: *A vocabulary-building exercise that focuses on furniture*

8 Grammar Focus: *Practices* there is/there are *and furniture vocabulary*

Interchange 7: *A fluency activity that reviews the vocabulary and grammar of this cycle*

9 Pronunciation: *Practices differentiating between* θ (**thir**teen) *and* ð (**the**)

10 Reading: *Practices reading for specific information*

WORKBOOK: Exercises 4–6 on pages 27 and 28

1️⃣ SNAPSHOT

SB p. 42 This activity introduces the theme of the unit by presenting information about the parts of a suburban home.

■ Books closed. On the board, draw a diagram like the following:

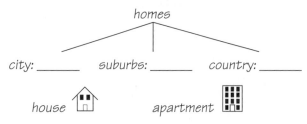

Then ask: "Where do people have apartments? Where do people have houses?" Fill in the blanks in the diagram.

■ Books open. Have students look at the picture. Ask them if it is a house or an apartment. Ask them if it is in the city, suburbs, or country. Students then read the Snapshot silently.

■ Read the discussion questions with the class. Then have students work alone to write the answers.

■ Students compare answers with a partner or in a small group. Ask several (or all) to share their responses with the class. Make a chart of their responses on the board:

Houses	Apartments
living room	living room
family room	------
bedrooms (3)	bedrooms (2)

2️⃣ CONVERSATION 📼

SB p. 42 This activity introduces short answers to present tense questions and expressions for talking about housing.

■ Books open. Students look at the picture. Say: "Linda has a new apartment. Listen."

■ Play the tape as students listen and read.

■ Present the conversation line by line. Explain or demonstrate that "Guess what?" = you have some news you want to tell, and that "no problem" is one of several responses to "Thank you"; it shows willingness to help.

■ Students practice the conversation in pairs using the Look Up and Say technique.

■ If you wish, have several pairs act out the conversation for the class.

3️⃣ GRAMMAR FOCUS: Present tense questions and short answers 📼

SB p. 43 This Grammar Focus practices present tense questions and short answers.

> **Grammar notes**
>
> 1. If necessary, review the rules for present tense questions presented in Unit 6, ex. 8, on page 58 of this Teacher's Manual.
>
> 2. Short answers to present tense questions use the auxiliary verb *do*, not the main verb: "Do you live here?" "Yes, I **do**." (*not* "Yes, I live.").

■ Books open. Play the tape or model the questions and answers in the box. Students listen and repeat.

■ If you wish, practice further by asking questions around the class: "Do you have a purple notebook? Do you have a pen?" etc.

1

■ Students work alone to complete the conversation with the appropriate verbs. (If students have trouble getting started, write "do," "have," and "live" on the board. The missing word will be a form of one of these verbs.)

■ Students compare their answers as a class, then practice the conversation in pairs.

■ As students practice, listen for intonation. Discuss problems as a class at the end.

Answers

Linda: Do you live in an apartment?
Chris: No, I don't. I live in a house.
Linda: What is it like? Does it have a yard?
Chris: Yes, it does. And it's next to the river.
Linda: That sounds great. Do you live alone?
Chris: No, I don't. I live with my parents and my
        sisters.
Linda: How many sisters do you have?
Chris: I have four.
Linda: That's a big family. Do you have a big
        house?
Chris: Yes, we do. It has ten rooms.
Linda: Ten rooms! How many bedrooms does it
        have?
Chris: It has four.
Linda: Do you have your own bedroom?
Chris: Yes, I do. I'm really lucky.
Linda: Does your bedroom have a view of the
        river?
Chris: No, it doesn't. It's in the basement.

2   Pair work

■ Students work alone to write five questions
about their partner's home. They can write
yes/no questions or wh-questions with *do*.

■ If necessary, get them started by telling the
class to ask you two questions about your home;
check for correct form and vocabulary.

■ Circulate to provide help and check for
accuracy. When most students seem finished,
pairs take turns asking and answering each
other's questions.

■ Bring the class back together and ask several
pairs to share a question and answer with the
class.

4   LISTENING 🔊

SB p. 43 This activity practices listening for the
gist of a description of a house or an apartment.

■ Books open. Look at the four pictures. Ask: "Is
this a house or an apartment? Where is it? What
room is this?" Elicit the word "ocean" for picture
(d).

■ Explain the task. Students will hear four short
monologues by different people. They are
describing where they live. Students match the
description to the picture.

■ Play the tape several times. Students number
the pictures from 1 to 4 as they listen.

■ If you wish, ask students to write down two key
words that helped them match the description to
the picture [e.g., for picture (a): "downtown,"
"city," "view"]. Discuss these words when you go
over the answers.

■ Have students compare their answers with a
partner; then go over the answers as a class.

■ Play the tape a final time so that students can
check their work.

Tape transcript

Listen to people describe their house or
apartment. Number the pictures from one to
four.

1)
WOMAN: My apartment is very small. It has just
        one room with a very small kitchen. It doesn't
        have a bedroom, so I sleep on the sofa. It's a
        studio apartment.

2)
MAN: I live next to the ocean. In fact, I have a
        view of the ocean from my living room. My
        house is very big. I have ten rooms.

3)
WOMAN: I live in an apartment downtown. It's a
        beautiful apartment. It has a big living room
        with a great view of the city. The view is really
        good at night.

4)
MAN: My family and I live in the country in a
        small house. We have a yard and a garden. My
        children play in the yard, and I work in the
        garden.

Answers

a) 3   b) 4   c) 1   d) 2

5 DREAM HOUSE

SB p. 44 This is a writing and speaking activity that reviews the grammar and vocabulary of the unit, and presents new vocabulary about homes.

1

■ Books open. Look at the photos and the sentences. Elicit the meaning of "dream house" by asking: "Where do you want to live? What kind of house do you want? Don't think about money."

■ Model the vocabulary in the photos; students repeat.

■ Students write their description.

2 Pair work

■ Explain the task and model the sample conversation by asking a student two questions (a yes/no question and a wh-question) about his or her dream house.

■ Students do the task in pairs, and take turns asking and answering.

■ Bring the class back together and ask several students to describe their dream house for the class.

■ If you wish, encourage students to use ideas brought up in the class discussion to revise or expand their paragraphs on their dream house. This can be an in-class writing activity or a homework assignment.

6 CONVERSATION 🔲

SB p. 44 This conversation introduces *there is/ there are* and vocabulary for talking about furnishings.

■ Books open. Play the tape as students listen and read. Ask students to underline any vocabulary they do not know.

■ Discuss vocabulary by encouraging students to figure out the meaning from context, and by using the illustration. (There is a picture of a yard sale on page 45 of the Student's Book.)

■ Present the conversation line by line; students repeat.

■ Students practice the conversation in pairs using the Look Up and Say technique.

■ If you wish, ask several pairs to act out the conversation for the class.

7 WORD POWER

SB p. 45 This activity expands vocabulary for household furnishings.

1

■ Books open. Look at the items in the picture, and model the words (or selected words). Students repeat.

■ Look at the chart and explain the task. If you wish, start the exercise as a class.

■ Students work alone to choose items for their new apartment and list the words in the appropriate columns.

Sample answers

(*Note:* The items are in alphabetical order. Many of these items can be used in more than one room. Suggested additional words for each list are at the end, in bold type.)

Kitchen	*Dining room*
microwave oven	chairs
refrigerator	table
stove	**candles**
dishwasher	**plants**
teapot	**tablecloth**
toaster	

Living room	*Bedroom*
armchairs	bed
bookcase	curtains
coffee table	desk
grandfather clock	dresser
rug	lamp
sofa	mirror
television	picture
piano	**clock**
stereo system	**radio**
telephone	**wastebasket**

2

■ Ask students to add three more things to each list. Circulate to help with vocabulary as students do this.

3   Pair work

■ Write this model dialogue on the board:

A: *For the kitchen, I need _____ . What do you need?*

B: *I need _____ . For the dining room, I need _____ . What do you need?*

■ Students compare lists in pairs, using the dialogue as a guide.

■ Bring the class back together and ask several students what they need at the yard sale. (Answers will vary.)

Extra practice

1. Tell students that you have a new home but no furniture. Draw a floor plan of a large house on the board and label the rooms. Have students call out the things they think you need and where they think these things should go:

S: You need a desk in your family room.

Either write the things students call out in the proper place in the floor plan, or have a student do this for you. (10 minutes)

2. Students work alone to list the furniture in their dream house from exercise 5. Then pairs compare lists like this:

A: Do you have a sofa?
B: Yes I do. I have three.
A: What's in the bedroom?
B: There's . . .

(10 minutes)

8 GRAMMAR FOCUS: *there is / there are*

SB p. 46 This Grammar Focus presents *there is / there are* with *some* and *any*.

Grammar note

Some is used in positive sentences, and *any* is used in negative sentences. If students need help understanding this, refer to the illustration in the Student's Book and write on the board:

There are some chairs in the living room, but there aren't any chairs in the kitchen.

Some and *any* are used with plural countable nouns. *A/an* and *no* are used with singular countable nouns. (All the nouns in this exercise are countable. See Unit 9 for examples of countable and uncountable nouns.)

■ Books open. Play the tape or model the sentences in the box. Students listen and repeat.

1   Pair work

■ Look at the picture of Linda's apartment. Ask the class to tell you some of the things they see and some of the things that aren't there. Use the model sentences in the book.

■ Students do the task in pairs.

■ Bring the class back together and ask several pairs to tell you one thing Linda has and one thing she doesn't have.

2   Pair work

■ Students write five sentences about things you have or don't have in your classroom.

■ Circulate to provide help and check for accuracy.

■ Have students compare sentences with a partner. Then ask several students to share one of their sentences with the class.

INTERCHANGE 7:
Find the differences

SB p. IC-10 This activity practices *there is/there are* and the vocabulary of the unit.

■ Books open to page IC-10. Explain the task and look at the pictures of Bill's and Jane's apartments, and go over the sample sentences.

■ Students work alone to write five more sentences about the differences between Jane's and Bill's apartments.

■ When most students have finished, have them compare sentences in pairs. Partners can practice saying their sentences like this:

A: There are three chairs in Jane's kitchen.
B: There are *four* chairs in Bill's kitchen.

Encourage students to stress the word that gives different information.

■ Bring the class back together and, if possible, give each student a chance to say one difference.

Extra practice

■ Students work alone to draw a picture of a room in their home and the things in it.

■ Pairs exchange drawings and talk about the differences between their rooms. Use the sentences in the Interchange Activity as a model. (10 minutes)

---

9 PRONUNCIATION:
/ð/ and /θ/ 🔊

SB p. 47 In this activity, students practice the contrast between voiced /ð/ and voiceless /θ/.

Pronunciation note

Voiceless *th* is made by putting the tongue behind the top teeth and blowing air. Voiced *th* is produced the same way, except the vocal cords vibrate. Students can place their fingers over their throat to feel the difference between the two sounds.

1

■ Books open. Play the tape or model the example sentence. Students listen, repeat, and practice. (If students have trouble distinguishing between the two sounds, model them rather than play the tape; the difference will be more apparent.)

2

■ Students work alone to list three more words with /ð/ and three more words with /θ/. If they need help in thinking of words, encourage them to use the Key Vocabulary lists for Units 1–7 at the back of their book, on pages V-2 to V-5.

■ Students compare lists in pairs and practice each other's words.

Sample answers

/ð/	/θ/
bathing suit	math
brother / mother / father	month
their	thank
them	thing
this / these	think
weather	Thursday

Optional activity: *Tongue twisters*

■ Pairs take turns saying these tongue twisters (= sentences with many similar sounds; they are hard to say). Have them start off slowly, then see how fast they can say them.

– There are thirty thick bath towels there in the bathroom.
– There is a store with three bathtubs, thirteen math books, thirty bathing suits, and other things on sale this Thursday.

(5–10 minutes)

🔟 READING 🔲

SB p. 47 This activity practices reading for specific information.

1

■ Books open. Look at the pictures of the three people. Ask: "What are they doing?"

■ Read the chart as a class. Make sure students understand the meaning of the headings. Tell students to read the descriptions and look for the answers.

■ If you wish, play the tape as students read the paragraphs for the first time. Then have students do the task individually.

■ Students compare their answers with a partner or as a class.

■ Go over the answers with the class.

Sample answers

(*Note:* Features may vary.)

Joseph Landi
Favorite room: kitchen
Activities: cooking/eating
Good features: big and modern

Liz Johnson
Favorite room: bedroom
Activities: reading / studying / playing computer
   games / sleeping
Good features: private

Susan Stern
Favorite room: living room
Activities: relaxing / watching TV / listening to
   music
Good features: beautiful pictures / comfortable
   sofa / relaxing

2

■ Students write five sentences about their favorite room. They can use the readings as models.

■ Students read their sentences to each other in pairs or small groups.

■ Ask several students to share their sentences with the class.

■ If you wish, students can turn these sentences into a short paragraph as an in-class activity or a homework assignment.

Extra practice

■ Ask students to remove their name from the paper on which they have written about their favorite room. Collect the papers and redistribute them randomly around the class. Students mingle and ask each other questions about the paragraph they have until they find the owner. For example: "Does your room have . . . ? Do you have a . . . ?" (10 minutes)

8 What do you do?

This unit has two cycles and focuses on the theme of jobs. It introduces
wh-questions with *do* and adjectives.

UNIT PLAN

Cycle 1

1 Word Power: *A vocabulary-building exercise on the topic of jobs*

2 Conversation: *Introduces wh-questions with* do *for talking about jobs*

3 Grammar Focus: *Offers fluency practice with wh-questions*

4 Pronunciation: *Practices falling intonation in wh-questions*

WORKBOOK: Exercises 1–3 on pages 29 to 31

Cycle 2

5 Snapshot: *Presents facts about salaries and job stress*

6 Conversation: *Introduces adjectives to describe jobs and salary*

7 Grammar Focus: *Practices adjectives and their opposites*

Interchange 8: *A fluency activity that reviews the grammar and vocabulary of the unit*

8 Listening: *Practices listening for the gist of a description of a job*

9 Reading: *Practices reading for specific information*

WORKBOOK: Exercises 4–6 on pages 31 and 32

1 WORD POWER 🔜

SB pp. 48–49 This activity presents vocabulary for the theme of this unit: occupations.

1

■ Books open. To illustrate "job" and "occupation," write on the board: "I'm a teacher. My job/occupation = teacher."

■ Model the words in the box; students repeat.

■ Explain the task: Students match the words in the box to the occupations in the pictures. List them in order from left to right. Students can use some occupations two times.

■ If you wish, students do the activity in pairs. If they get stuck on vocabulary, they can use their dictionaries.

■ Have students compare their answers with a partner or as a class. Then play the tape so that students can check their work.

■ Play the tape again; students listen and repeat.

Tape transcript with answers

a) She's a receptionist.
b) She's a doctor.
c) She's a nurse.
d) She's a musician.
e) She's a singer.
f) He's a musician.
g) He's a chef.
h) He's a waiter.
i) She's a waitress.
j) He's a pilot.
k) She's a flight attendant.
l) He's a flight attendant.
m) She's a judge.
n) He's a lawyer.
o) He's a police officer.
p) He's a security guard.
q) He's a salesclerk.
r) He's a cashier.

2 Pair work

■ Books open. Explain the task: Pairs of students name the people who work at each place using the list of occupations on page 48. Model the sample language. (Students can use some occupations in two lists.)

■ Pairs write occupations under the correct pictures. Then, using their dictionaries if necessary, they add one more occupation to each list.

■ Call on students to report their answers to the class. Encourage them to use the language in the model. Create a class list on the board.

Sample answers

(*Note:* These answers use words from page 48 only; words for additional occupations will vary.)

In a hospital: receptionist, doctor, nurse
In an office: receptionist, lawyer, doctor
In a store: salesclerk, cashier, security guard
In a hotel: receptionist, cashier, security guard, cook/chef, waiter/waitress

3 Class activity

■ Read the list of questions with the class and discuss any vocabulary that presents problems. Use gestures or the pictures in the book to explain "uniform," "money," "gun," "stand," "sit," and "hard."

■ Model the example dialogue with a student.

■ If your class is large, divide into groups of eight to ten to do the activity. Ask and answer questions around the class. Answers will vary (e.g., police officers carry guns in some countries but not in others).

2 CONVERSATION 🔊

SB p. 49 This conversation introduces wh-questions with *do* to ask about occupations.

■ Books open. Students look at the picture. Ask what jobs the two men do. (Answers: security guard and chef)

■ Play the tape; students listen and read.

■ Present the conversation line by line; students repeat.

■ Students practice in pairs using the Look Up and Say technique.

■ If you wish, ask pairs to perform for the class.

3 GRAMMAR FOCUS:
Present tense: Wh-questions with *do* 🔊

SB p. 50 This Grammar Focus practices present tense wh-questions with *do* that ask about people's occupations.

Grammar notes

1. If necessary, review present tense question formation (see page 58, Unit 6, ex. 8, grammar notes, of this Teacher's Manual).

2. Note the two uses of *do* in this question: "What *does* she *do* there?" *Does* is the auxiliary verb; it is in third person singular to agree with the subject ("she"). *Do* is the main verb and carries the most important meaning in the sentence; it is in the base form.

■ Books open. Play the tape or model the sentences in the box. Students listen and read.

■ Play the tape again; students listen and repeat.

1

■ Explain the task: It has two parts. First, students complete the sentences with the correct verb form. Then they put the sentences in order to make a conversation.

■ Students do the task individually.

■ Have students compare their answers in pairs. Then play the tape so that students can check their answers.

■ Students practice the conversations in pairs.

Tape transcript with answers

a) Where <u>does</u> Elizabeth <u>work</u>?
   She <u>works</u> in a hospital.
   Really? What <u>does</u> she <u>do</u> there?
   She<u>'s</u> a doctor.

b) Where <u>do</u> you <u>work</u>?
   I <u>work</u> in a department store.
   Oh? And what <u>do</u> you <u>do</u> there?
   I<u>'m</u> a salesperson. I <u>sell</u> computers.

c) What <u>does</u> Tom <u>do</u>?
   He <u>works</u> in an electronics store.
   What <u>does</u> he do there, exactly?
   He <u>repairs</u> TVs.

2 Class activity

■ Students stand and ask three different classmates about their occupation.

Note: If your students do not have jobs, they can identify themselves as students, like this:

A: Where do you work?
B: I don't have a job. I'm a student.
A: What do you study, exactly?
B: I study English/languages/(etc.).

Help with vocabulary as needed.

■ Bring the class back together; students report their findings to the class using the sentence in their book as a model.

4 PRONUNCIATION: Falling intonation ▭▭

SB p. 50 This activity practices falling intonation in wh-questions and short answers.

> **Pronunciation note**
>
> Wh-questions always end with falling intonation. This contrasts with yes/no questions, which always end with rising intonation. (See Unit 5, ex. 8, on page 50 of this Teacher's Manual for more on intonation and pitch.)

1

■ Books open. Play the tape or model the four sentences. Students listen and read.

■ Play the tape or model the sentences again. This time students listen and repeat.

■ If necessary, hum the sentences so that students can focus on the change in pitch (intonation).

2

■ Students look again at the three conversations in part 1 of exercise 3, Grammar Focus. Tell students: "Listen to the falling intonation."

■ Rewind the tape to part 1 of exercise 3. Play the tape as students listen. Then have pairs practice the conversations, paying attention to intonation.

5 SNAPSHOT

SB p. 51 This activity presents some interesting facts about salaries and jobs in the U.S.

■ Books closed. List all of the jobs from the Snapshot on the board in random order:

____ *airline pilot*   ____ *college professor*
____ *police officer*   ____ *receptionist*
____ *nurse*   ____ *air traffic controller*
____ *doctor*   ____ *restaurant cook*
____ *travel agent*   ____ *high school teacher*
____ *lawyer*

■ Working in pairs, students order the jobs from highest to lowest salary. Explain that "salary" = the money you get for doing a job.

■ If you wish, ask students to divide the jobs into two lists: "stressful" and "not stressful." If necessary, illustrate "stress" by having students looking at the picture in exercise 6 on page 51: The air traffic controller has a very stressful job.

■ Ask a few pairs to share their guesses with the class.

■ Books open. Students read the information in the Snapshot and compare it to their own guesses.

■ Read the two discussion questions with the class. Students work alone to write answers.

■ Students compare their answers as a class.

■ Ask students what jobs have high/low stress and high/low salaries in their own countries. Are they the same or different?

6   CONVERSATION 🔲

SB p. 51 This conversation presents adjectives and expressions for talking about work.

■ Books open. Students cover the text with a piece of paper. Look at the picture and ask: "Where does the man work? What does he do?"

■ Books closed. On the board write: "What does Stephanie do? Where does she work?"

■ Play the tape; students listen for the answers. Ask students to answer the questions. (Answers: Stephanie is a teacher. She teaches math at a high school.)

■ Books open. Play the tape again as students follow along in their books.

■ Present the conversation line by line; students repeat. Explain that "not bad" means "OK," or "not bad but not good."

■ Students practice the conversation in pairs. Encourage them to use falling intonation at the end of sentences.

■ If you wish, ask for pairs of students to act out their conversation for the class. They can substitute their own information.

---

7   GRAMMAR FOCUS:
Adjectives 🔲

SB p. 52 This Grammar Focus presents *be* + adjectives and adjectives + nouns as well as adjectives with opposite meanings.

■ Books open. Play the tape or model the sentences and opposites in the boxes. Students listen and read.

■ Play the tape again; students repeat.

■ If necessary, illustrate the concept of "opposites" like this. Write on the board:

Easy	Difficult
$2 \times 2 = $ ___	$(187.99 \times 37.8)^2 \div 6 = $ ___

Explain that the opposite of "easy" is "difficult." Illustrate "high" and "low" as well, using the salary chart on page 51.

■ Ask students to find one or two adjectives in the list to describe the jobs depicted in the photos on page 52.

1

■ Explain the task by reading the example as a class. Students change the sentences to adjective + noun form. They need to pay attention to meaning because they may have to use a different adjective when they change the sentence.

■ Go around the class and have students do the task orally, or have them work individually and write the answers.

■ Go over the answers with the class.

Answers

b) A computer programmer has a difficult job.
c) A doctor has a high salary.
d) A lawyer has a difficult job. (*or* A lawyer doesn't have an easy job.)
e) A chef has a pleasant job.
f) A security guard has a dangerous job.

2   Pair work

■ Explain the task: Students write adjectives in the sentences. They write their own opinion; there are no correct or incorrect answers. Do the first sentence as an example if necessary.

■ Students do the task individually.

■ Have students compare answers in pairs. Then ask each student to share one sentence with the class. Do the other students agree?

3   Class activity

■ Read the chart as a class. Then have students work individually and write two jobs for each category. They write their own opinion.

■ Go around the class and ask each student to name a job from one of the categories. Students who agree say the sentence another way:

T: Who has an exciting job?
S1: A musician has an exciting job.
T: [*to another student*] Do you agree?
S2: No, I think a musician has a boring job. (*or* Yes, I agree. A musician's job is exciting.)

INTERCHANGE 8:
The perfect job

`SB p. IC-11` In this communication activity, students use present tense questions and answers to talk about jobs.

1 Pair work

■ Books open to page IC-11. Elicit the meaning of "perfect job" (= your "dream" job; a job you like very much). Ask students to read the list of questions in the chart and circle any vocabulary they do not know. Use the pictures and captions to help illustrate vocabulary. Note that *want to* + verb is used as a formula here. It is taught in Unit 16.

■ In the "Me" column, students check "yes" or "no" for each question. They work individually and write their own opinion.

■ In pairs, students take turns asking and answering the questions. They write their partner's answers in their books.

■ If you wish, take a class survey with a show of hands for each question. Students can take turns asking the questions to the rest of the class. Tally the results on the board.

2 Class activity

■ Explain the task: "Think of a job for yourself. Think about the answers on your job survey." Give students a few minutes to think of a job and their reasons.

■ Model the sample language about the person who wants to be a musician.

■ Go around the class and give each student a chance to talk about his or her perfect job. In larger classes, do this step in groups of eight to ten.

Extra practice

■ Pairs discuss a job they do not want to do: "I don't want to be a teacher because I don't want to . . . " When pairs have finished, bring the class back together and have students report their conclusions.

8 LISTENING

`SB p. 53` This activity practices listening for the gist of a description of a job.

■ Books open. Look at the four pictures. Ask: "Where does this woman work? What does she do?"

■ Explain the task: Students listen to four short conversations. Women are talking about their jobs. Students match the job in the conversation to the correct picture.

■ Play the tape several times; students perform the task.

■ If you wish, ask students to write down key words in each conversation that gave them the answer. For example, in conversation (1): "hotel," "cashier," "money."

■ Have students compare answers and key words with a partner. Then go over the answers as a class.

■ Play the tape a final time to confirm answers.

Tape transcript

Listen to these women talk about their jobs. Number the pictures from one to four.

1)
A: Where do you work now, Theresa?
B: I have a job at a hotel. It's great.
A: What do you do, exactly?
B: I'm a cashier. I handle all the money.
A: Wow! That's exciting.

2)
A: What do you do, Cecilia?
B: I work in a restaurant.
A: Really. What do you do, exactly?
B: I'm a chef. I cook lunch and dinner there.
A: That's not an easy job, is it?
B: No, it's a difficult job, but I like it.

(transcript continues on next page)

3)

A: Where do you work, Christine?
B: At a French restaurant.
A: Uh, are you a chef? A waitress?
B: No, actually, I'm a singer. I sing with a band there at night.

4)

A: What do you do, Kathleen?
B: I work for Transnational Airlines.
A: Oh, are you a flight attendant?
B: No, I'm a pilot.
A: Now that's a stressful job.
B: Yeah, but I really like the work.

Answers

a) 4   b) 2   c) 1   d) 3

---

9 READING 🔊

SB p. 53 This activity practices reading for specific information.

1

■ Books open. Point out the chart. Tell students that they read about three jobs to find out information for the chart. Then have students read the three job descriptions silently.

■ Students complete the chart individually. Reassure them that they do not need to understand every word in order to do the task. *Note:* Students should be able to find the answers from the first two paragraphs without any vocabulary help. The third paragraph has several challenging words, but encourage students to do the task without using a dictionary.

■ Students share their answers with the class. Discuss any questions about vocabulary.

■ If you wish, after students have done the task, play the tape as students listen and read.

Answers

Anthony Duran
Job: telephone operator/directory assistance operator
Salary: $20,000 a year
What he does: gives out telephone numbers
One good thing about the job: talking to people

Robert Fine
Job: travel agent
Salary: $24,000 a year
What he does: makes reservations for people
One good thing about the job: secure/free travel

Kimberly Evans
Job: physical therapist
Salary: $38,000 a year
What she does: works with athletes who have sports injuries
One good thing about the job: works with famous athletes/good salary/a lot of patients

2

■ Explain the task: Students write five sentences about their job. If they do not work, they can write about their "perfect job" from Interchange 8.

■ Students do the task individually.

■ Have students compare their work in small groups or pairs. Then bring the class back together, and ask several students to read their sentences to the class.

■ If you wish, students can turn their sentences into a short paragraph as an in-class or homework assignment.

Optional activity: *What's this job?*

■ Students choose one of the jobs listed in the Snapshot or the Word Power activity. They write five sentences about the job without mentioning the name. For example:

"I work in an office. I don't wear a uniform. My salary is average. My job is not stressful. I answer the telephone and greet people."

■ Students form groups and take turns reading their sentences aloud. The other students guess the job. (10–15 minutes)

Review of Units 5–8

This unit reviews the vocabulary of time, daily schedules, housing, transportation, and jobs. It also focuses on the present continuous, simple present, and *there is/there are.*

UNIT PLAN

1 Listening: *Practices listening for specific information and reviews time expressions and the present continuous*

2 Different Responses: *Fluency practice in talking about activities with the present continuous*

3 Habits: *Reviews use of the simple present to talk about habitual actions*

4 Comparisons: *Reviews vocabulary about housing and* there is/ there are

5 What's the Question?: *Reviews wh-questions in the simple present and present continuous*

---

1 LISTENING 🔘

SB p. 54 This activity practices listening for specific information. It reviews time expressions and the present continuous tense.

■ Books open. Look at the four pictures and model the names. Explain the task: Victoria is calling friends in different parts of the world. Students hear three short telephone conversations. They listen for the three pieces of information requested in the chart.

■ Play the tape several times while students complete the chart. If students have difficulty, have them listen only for the city during the first playing, the time during the second playing, and the activity during the third playing. Then play the tape a fourth time so that they can check their answers.

■ Have students compare their answers with a partner. Then go over the answers as a class.

■ Play the tape a final time so that students can confirm the correct answers.

Tape transcript

Pair work Victoria is calling friends in different parts of the world. Where are they? What time is it there? What are they doing? Complete the chart.

[*phone rings*]
SUE: Hello?
VICTORIA: Hello, Sue? This is Victoria. I'm calling from Los Angeles.
SUE: Oh, hi, Victoria.
VICTORIA: So, how are things in New York City?
SUE: Fine, just fine.
VICTORIA: By the way, what time is it in New York?
SUE: It's twelve o'clock.
VICTORIA: It's noon? Oh. Are you having lunch?
SUE: No, I'm watching television.
VICTORIA: Oh. What are you watching?
SUE: The news. Right now they're giving the . . . [*fades out*]

(transcript continues on next page)

[*phone rings*]

JUAN: Bueno?

VICTORIA: Hello, Juan? This is Victoria, from Los Angeles. How are you?

JUAN: I'm not sure, Victoria. I'm not very awake.

VICTORIA: Oh, what time is it in Mexico City?

JUAN: Well, it's a quarter after eleven in the morning here.

VICTORIA: Eleven fifteen A.M.?

JUAN: Yes, and I'm having breakfast.

VICTORIA: You're having breakfast?

JUAN: Right. I always sleep late on Saturdays, you know . . . [*fades out*]

[*phone rings*]

JIM: Hello?

VICTORIA: Is this Jim?

JIM: Yes, it is. Who's calling, please?

VICTORIA: This is Victoria. I'm calling from Los Angeles.

JIM: Oh, hi, Victoria.

VICTORIA: So, how are things in Sydney?

JIM: Things are fine here, but you know it's three thirty in the morning.

VICTORIA: Oh, am I calling at a bad time?

JIM: Luckily, no. I'm not sleeping. I'm reading a book about a detective . . . [*fades out*]

Answers

	City	Time	Activity
Sue	New York	noon/ 12:00 P.M.	watching TV
Juan	Mexico City	11:15 A.M.	having breakfast
Jim	Sydney	3:30 A.M.	reading a book

2 | DIFFERENT RESPONSES

SB p. 54 This activity reviews the present continuous tense.

■ Books open. Explain the task: Students answer the questions two different ways, using the present continuous. There are three new words that you may want to explain or illustrate before you begin: "course," "noise," and "party." Read the questions with the class, and discuss any problems with vocabulary.

■ Students write their answers individually.

■ Students work in pairs and take turns asking and answering the questions.

■ Bring the class back together and ask several pairs to share their most interesting question and answer with the class.

Extra practice

■ Students work with a partner to write three more questions in the present continuous like those in the exercise.

■ Pairs exchange questions and take turns asking and answering them. (10 minutes)

3 | HABITS

SB p. 55 This activity reviews the use of the present tense for habitual actions.

■ Books open. Explain the task: Students write eight sentences about their lives. Read the list of questions with the class.

■ Students answer the questions individually. If they have trouble getting started, write some sentences as a class, or use some of the sample answers below.

■ Students compare answers with a partner.

■ Bring the class back together, and have several students answer one of the questions for the class.

Sample answers

a) I get dressed in the morning. I have breakfast in the morning.

b) I don't have lunch in the morning. I don't go to class in the morning.

c) I watch TV on the weekend. I go running on the weekend.

d) I don't work on the weekend. I don't clean the house on the weekend.

4 COMPARISONS

`SB p. 55` This activity reviews *there is/there are*.

■ Books open. Begin with a brainstorming activity. Students call out differences between a house and an apartment; write them on the board. For example:

House	Apartment
yard	no yard
garage	no garage
basement	no basement
garden	no garden

Repeat this process for city/country. For example:

City	Country
apartments	houses
public transportation	cars
no yards	yards
schools	no schools

■ Model the sample sentence in the book, and tell students to write four sentences about the differences between a house and an apartment, and then between the city and the country. Have students use the expressions in the box.

■ Students work individually.

■ Ask each student to share a difference with the class or in small groups.

5 WHAT'S THE QUESTION?

`SB p. 55` This activity reviews present tense questions.

1

■ Books open. Read sentence (a) as a class. Ask: "What's the question?" ("Where do you work?").

■ Students work individually and write a suitable question for each answer.

■ Students compare their questions with a partner. Then go over them as a class. (Answers will vary; accept any reasonable answer.)

Sample answers

b) What do you do?
I'm a salesclerk.

c) Do you like your job? / How do you like your job?
I really like my job.

d) Where do you live?
I live in an apartment downtown.

e) How many rooms does your apartment (do you) have? / Do you have a big apartment? / Is your apartment big?
My apartment has a kitchen, a bathroom, and a living room.

f) What does your apartment need? / What (furniture) do you need?
I need a sofa, a rug, and a carpet.

g) Do you like your English class?
I think my English class is great!

h) How do you go to class?
I go to class by subway.

i) What time do you get up (in the morning)?
I get up at 6:00 A.M. every morning.

j) What time is it?
It's four o'clock in the morning!

k) What are you doing?
I'm watching television right now.

2   Pair work

■ Books open. Explain the task: Students use the questions they wrote for part 1. They ask their partner the questions, and the partner answers with real information (not with the sentences in the book). If necessary, model the task by having a student ask you the first two questions; you answer them.

■ Students take turns asking and answering the questions with their partner.

■ Ask each pair to share a question and answer with the class.

9 I love strawberries!

This unit has two cycles. The theme of the unit is food, and it practices the language of meals, shopping lists, and ingredients. The focus is on countable and uncountable nouns, word stress, *some* and *any*, and adverbs of frequency.

UNIT PLAN

Cycle 1

1 Word Power: *A vocabulary-building exercise on names and categories of foods*

2 Grammar Focus: *Introduces and practices countable and uncountable nouns in the context of food likes and dislikes*

3 Pronunciation: *Practices word stress with food vocabulary*

4 Conversation: *Introduces* some *and* any *and more food names*

5 Listening: *Practices listening for detail about shopping lists*

6 Grammar Focus: *Practices using* some *and* any

WORKBOOK: Exercises 1–5 on pages 33 to 35

Cycle 2

7 Snapshot: *Presents traditional breakfasts from around the world*

8 Conversation: *Introduces expressions for talking about meals and adverbs of frequency*

9 Grammar Focus: *Fluency practice with adverbs of frequency*

10 Reading: *Practices reading a description of the hamburger for the main idea and for detail*

Interchange 9: *A fluency activity that practices the vocabulary and grammar of the unit*

WORKBOOK: Exercises 6–8 on pages 35 and 36

1 WORD POWER

SB p. 56 This activity introduces students to the vocabulary of some basic food types by having them match illustrations of foods to the corresponding words.

■ Books open. Explain the task: Students match the pictures to the words in the chart. If you wish, model the words in the chart before students do the task.

■ Students do the task in pairs. Students are not expected to match all of the words.

■ When they have matched as many as they can, play the tape. As students listen, they check their answers and fill in any words they did not know.

■ When they have finished, play the tape again; students listen and repeat.

■ Students add two more words to each list. Write the five food categories on the board. Students create a class list by coming to the board and writing the foods they added to each category.

Tape Transcript

Match the foods to the words in the chart. Then listen and practice. Add two more foods to each category.

a) These are bananas.
b) These are oranges.
c) These are apples.
d) These are strawberries.
e) These are mangoes.
f) These are carrots.
g) These are tomatoes.
h) This is broccoli.
i) These are green beans.
j) These are peppers.
k) This is pasta.
l) This is bread.
m) These are beans.
n) This is rice.
o) These are potatoes.
p) This is milk.
q) These are eggs.
r) This is cheese.
s) This is butter.
t) This is yogurt.

u) This is chicken.
v   This is beef.
w) This is lamb.
x) This is shrimp.
y) This is salmon.

Answers

Fruit
c apples
a bananas
e mangoes
b oranges
d strawberries

Vegetables
h broccoli
f carrots
i green beans
j peppers
g tomatoes

Starches
m beans
l bread
k pasta
o potatoes
n rice

Dairy
s butter
r cheese
q eggs
p milk
t yogurt

Meat and fish
v beef
u chicken
w lamb
y salmon
x shrimp

2 GRAMMAR FOCUS:
Countable vs. uncountable

SB p. 57 This Grammar Focus presents and contrasts countable and uncountable nouns using the vocabulary of food.

> **Grammar note**
>
> The concept of countable and uncountable nouns is likely to be difficult for some students, as the distinction does not exist in all languages, and if it does exist, nouns that are countable in English may be uncountable in another language. Moreover, some nouns may be both countable and uncountable in English (e.g., chicken). This activity introduces the concept of countable and uncountable nouns in a way that is easy for students to understand. It is not necessary at this point to discuss exceptions to the rule.

■ Books open. Play the tape or model the words and sentences in the box. Students listen and repeat.

(instructions continue on next page)

■ Using the example sentences, point out that uncountable nouns are always in the singular. They do not, however, take the articles *a* or *an* (e.g., "I'm eating yogurt."). Countable nouns may be in the singular or plural; they take the article *a* or *an* in the singular (e.g., "I'm eating an apple."). Countable nouns are in the plural in general statements (e.g., "Apples are delicious. I love apples.").

1

■ Explain the task: Students look back at the chart on page 56 of their book and divide the words into countable and uncountable nouns. Students write the words in the appropriate list in the chart on page 57.

■ If necessary, point out that the countable nouns in the lists on page 56 have a plural *s* at the end of the word, but the uncountable nouns do not.

■ Students do the task individually. If they have trouble, classify a few of the words as a class.

■ Have students compare their answers with a partner; then go over them as a class.

Answers

Countable	*Uncountable*
apples	broccoli
bananas	bread
mangoes	pasta
oranges	rice
strawberries	butter
carrots	cheese
green beans	milk
peppers	yogurt
tomatoes	beef
beans	chicken
potatoes	lamb
eggs	salmon
	shrimp

2 Pair work

■ Students cover the chart at the bottom of page 56 and then identify the foods. Model the sample language before they begin.

3

■ Explain the task: Students decide whether the noun is countable or uncountable (in this case, plural or singular), and then write the appropriate verb form. (*Note:* This task is not difficult. It is intended to help students remember that countable nouns are always in the plural in general statements.)

■ Students do the task individually.

■ Have students compare answers with a partner. Then play the tape so they can check their work.

■ Students practice saying the sentences in pairs. Elicit the meanings of "love" and "hate."

Tape transcript with answers

a) Strawberries <u>are</u> my favorite fruit. I love strawberries!
b) I think mangoes <u>are</u> delicious.
c) Green beans <u>are</u> my favorite vegetable.
d) Broccoli <u>is</u> very good for you.
e) I think cheese <u>is</u> awful. I hate cheese!
f) Chicken <u>is</u> my favorite meat.

4 Pair work

■ Explain the task and read through the questions with the class. Point out the sample language in the box.

■ Students work individually to write their answers.

■ Model the sample conversation and ask students to share their responses with a partner.

■ Bring the class back together and ask several students to share some of their answers with the class.

Alternative presentation

■ Take a poll of the foods students love and the foods they hate. Tally the results on the board:

I love . . .	I hate . . .
mangoes	chicken
yogurt	bananas

3 PRONUNCIATION: Word stress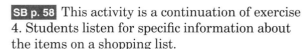

SB p. 58 This activity practices word stress patterns.

■ Play the tape or model the words. Students first listen and read then listen and repeat.

■ If necessary, review syllables (see pp. 31–32, Unit 3, ex. 6, of this Teacher's Manual). Ask students how many syllables each word has.

■ Students look at the list of foods on page 56 of their book and find one more word to match each pattern.

■ Ask several students to say the words they have found. Then the class repeats these words.

Answers

Many words are stressed on the first syllable, so answers will vary. "Bananas" is the only additional word on page 56 with the stress on the second syllable.

Extra practice

■ Read the words in the chart in exercise 1. Students listen and write a "1" next to the words stressed on the first syllable and a "2" next to the words stressed on the second syllable. (All are stressed on the first syllable except the following: bananas, tomatoes, potatoes.)

---

4 CONVERSATION 🔊

SB p. 58 This conversation introduces statements and questions with *some* and *any*, and introduces new food vocabulary.

■ Books open. Students look at the picture and call out the food items they see. Ask: "What are the people doing?"

■ Play the tape as students listen and read.

■ Present the conversation line by line; students repeat.

■ Students practice the conversation in pairs, using the Look Up and Say technique.

■ If you wish, ask several pairs to act out the conversation for the class.

5 LISTENING 🔊

SB p. 58 This activity is a continuation of exercise 4. Students listen for specific information about the items on a shopping list.

■ Books open. Explain the task: Anne and Charles are continuing their conversation from exercise 4. They are choosing desserts now. Students read the shopping list and listen for the two desserts.

■ Look at the illustration. Elicit the names of the desserts from the class.

■ Play the tape two or three times. Students complete the shopping list as they listen.

■ Students compare answers with a partner. If necessary, play the tape a final time so that students can confirm their answers.

Tape transcript

Listen to the rest of the conversation. Which desserts do Charles and Anne choose? Complete their shopping list.

CHARLES: Let's not forget dessert.
ANNE: Yeah. How about some fruit? Maybe mangoes and strawberries.
CHARLES: Hm. I don't really like fruit.
ANNE: I know. Your favorite dessert is apple pie.
CHARLES: Yes. Apple pie with ice cream.
ANNE: OK. So let's put apple pie and ice cream on the shopping list.

Answers

apple pie
ice cream

6 GRAMMAR FOCUS:
some, any 🔊

SB p. 59 This Grammar Focus practices *some* in affirmative statements and *any* in questions and negative statements.

> **Grammar note**
> *Some* and *any* are used with plural countable nouns ("vegetables") and singular uncountable nouns ("meat").

■ Books open. Play the tape or model the sentences in the box. Students listen and read.

■ Play the tape or model the language again. Students repeat and practice the sentences.

■ To make sure students understand the difference between *some* and *any*, write these sentences on the board and ask students to fill in the blanks:

> I have _____ vegetables.
> Do you have _____ carrots?

1
■ Have students name the items shown in the photo (*clockwise:* mayonnaise, potatoes, celery, onions, and carrots).

■ Students work individually to complete the conversation with *some* or *any*.

■ Have students compare their answers with a partner. Then go over the answers with the class.

Answers

Charles: Let's not buy potato salad. Let's make some.
Anne: OK. So we need some potatoes and some mayonnaise.
Charles: Is there any mayonnaise at home?
Anne: No, we need to buy some.
Charles: OK. Oh, we need some onions, too.
Anne: I don't want any onions in the salad. I hate onions!
Charles: Then let's buy some celery. That's good in potato salad.
Anne: Good idea. And some carrots, too.
Charles: Sure. There are some over there.

2 Pair work
■ Explain the task and model the sample language. Then pairs talk about what they need from the supermarket today.

Optional activity: *Shopping lists*

■ Write the names of two or three simple dishes on the board that all students are likely to know how to make.

■ Tell students to imagine they have nothing in the refrigerator. Ask: "What do you need from the supermarket?"

■ Students work in pairs and talk about what they need to buy from the supermarket. Circulate around the class to provide help with vocabulary. (10 minutes)

7 SNAPSHOT

SB p. 59 This activity builds schema and interest by presenting information about traditional breakfasts in the U.S., Japan, and Mexico.

■ Books closed. Ask several students: "What do you eat for breakfast?" Students respond simply.

■ Then ask, "What do you think is a traditional breakfast in the United States?" If necessary, explain that "tradition" = an old custom.

■ Students work alone or in pairs and list the foods they think people in the U.S. eat for breakfast.

■ Books open. Students read the information in the Snapshot. Ask about the students' predictions. Did students guess the right foods?

■ Ask students some questions about traditional breakfasts in Japan and Mexico, such as: "Does a traditional Japanese breakfast have meat? Do Mexicans eat eggs for breakfast?" Point out that most people do not eat traditional breakfasts on a daily basis, but rather on special occasions.

■ Read the discussion questions with the class. Students work alone to answer the questions and then share their answers with the class. Alternatively, do this as a class activity (especially if you think students will need help with vocabulary).

8 CONVERSATION 🔇

SB p. 60 This activity presents adverbs of frequency in a conversation about a traditional Japanese breakfast.

■ Books open. Students cover the text and look at the illustration. Explain that Kumiko and Sarah are talking about breakfast.

■ Books closed. On the board write: "When does Kumiko's family have a traditional Japanese breakfast?"

■ Play the tape once or twice; students listen to answer the question. Then ask the class to answer as a group. (Answer: on Sundays) Explain that "on Sundays" means "every Sunday."

■ Books open. Play the tape as students listen and read.

■ Present the conversation line by line; students repeat. Contrast "on Sunday," which means "this Sunday," with "on Sundays," which means "every Sunday."

■ Students practice the conversation in pairs using the Look Up and Say technique.

■ If you wish, ask pairs to act out the conversation for the class.

Extra practice

■ Pairs practice the conversation again, this time using information about what their own families have for breakfast on Sundays. (5 minutes)

9 GRAMMAR FOCUS: Frequency adverbs 🔇

SB p. 60 This activity practices adverbs of frequency in questions and answers.

> **Grammar note**
>
> The adverbs of frequency presented in this activity are placed after the subject (and auxiliary *do*) and before the main verb. Although exceptions to this word order exist in English, ignore these for the time being so that students can learn this pattern.

■ Books open. Play the tape or model the language in the box. Students listen and read.

■ Point out the box to the right. It illustrates the meaning of the adverbs of frequency.

■ Play the tape or model the language again. Students listen and repeat.

1

■ Students do the task individually, writing the sentences on a separate sheet of paper.

■ Students compare answers with a partner.

■ Go over the answers with the class. Then pairs practice the conversation.

Answers

A: What do you usually have for breakfast?
B: Well, I often have eggs, bacon, and toast on Sundays.
A: Do you ever eat breakfast at work?
B: Yes, I sometimes have breakfast at my desk.
A: Do you ever eat rice for breakfast?
B: I don't often have rice.

(instructions continue on next page)

2   Pair work

■ Explain the task and read through the list of questions with the class.

■ Students write three more questions of their own.

■ Pairs take turns asking and answering the questions.

■ Bring the class back together and have several pairs share their most interesting question and answer with the class.

Extra practice

■ Write the name of a meal on the board and say a frequency adverb. Ask students to talk about the meal using the frequency adverb. They should give real information. After a few students have responded, change the frequency adverb. For example:

T: [*writes "lunch"*] Always.
S1: I always have soup for lunch.
S2: I always have lunch at work.
S3: I always drink milk for lunch.

T: Never.
S1: I never have meat for lunch. (etc.)

■ When students run out of things to say, change the name of the meal.

10   READING 🔲

SB p. 61 This activity practices both reading for gist and reading for detail in a description of the hamburger.

1

■ Books open. Look at the picture and ask: "Do you ever eat hamburgers?"

■ Explain the task: Students read the text silently to match the letters in the pictures to the corresponding paragraphs.

■ If you wish, play the tape as students read.

■ Students compare answers with a partner and then as a class.

Answers

c̲ The **hamburger** is made of beef, not ham. . . .
d̲ The **pickle**, or pickled cucumber, comes from Eastern Europe. . . .
e̲ The word **ketchup** comes from China. . . .
b̲ **Mayonnaise**, sometimes called "mayo," is a yellow-white sauce . . .
a̲ The **bun** is a kind of bread. . . .

2

■ Before doing question (a), elicit the meaning of "ingredients" from the class using the illustration of the hamburger.

■ Write the chart on the board and ask the class to name the ingredients of a hamburger and the place or places of origin. If you wish, students can do the task in pairs.

Answers

Ingredient	*Place(s) of origin*
chopped beef	Turkey and Hamburg, Germany
pickle	Eastern Europe (e.g., Poland, Russia)
ketchup	China, the United States
mayonnaise	Minorca, Spain (but the name comes from France)
bun	England (but the sesame seeds come from the Middle East)

■ For question (b), ask students to name other things they like to put on hamburgers. List their answers on the board.

Possible answers

bacon	lettuce
cheese	mustard
green (or hot) peppers	onions
salt, pepper	tomato

■ Before students do the writing task in part (c), ask them to think of their favorite sandwich, snack, or dessert. Have them write the name and list the ingredients on a piece of paper.

■ Write these questions on the board:

1. *What is the name of your favorite sandwich, snack, or dessert?*
2. *What ingredients do you need?*
3. *How do you make it? (What do you do first? second? etc.)*

Tell students to write a paragraph that answers these questions in order. This can be done as an in-class activity or as homework.

■ When students have finished their paragraph, ask them to show it to a partner. Partners read each other's paragraph and ask questions if they do not understand something.

■ Have students revise their paragraphs based on their partner's comments. Then students can hand in their paragraph or read them aloud to the rest of the class.

Optional activities

1. Students take turns reading a description of their favorite snack, sandwich, or dessert to the class – without mentioning the name of the food. The class guesses the name of the food.

2. Students write sentences to describe the worst sandwich they can imagine. For example: "This sandwich is made of peanut butter and tofu. It has pickles and mayonnaise. You put it on a bun."

■ Students read their descriptions to each other in small groups or as a class. The class votes on the "worst" sandwich.

INTERCHANGE 9:
Planning a picnic

SB p. IC-12 This extension activity provides a good review of all of the grammar and vocabulary presented in the unit.

1 Group work

■ Books open to page IC-12. Explain the task and model the expressions.

■ Divide the class into small groups. Students ask and answer questions about foods in order to complete the chart.

2

■ Explain the task and model the expressions. Then groups decide upon a menu for the picnic. Everyone has to agree.

3 Class activity

■ Students mingle and compare menus.

■ Bring the class back together and have each group present their menu to the class. The class votes on the best menu.

Optional activity

■ Tell the class: "Let's have a class party." The class decides upon a single menu they all can enjoy. Have students call out the things they want to eat and drink, and list these on the board.

10 Can you swim very well?

This unit has two cycles and focuses on the theme of abilities, particularly sports. It presents *can* and *can't* for talking about abilities, as well as the expressions *know how to* and *be good at*.

UNIT PLAN

Cycle 1

1 Snapshot: *Introduces the theme of sports*

2 Conversation: *Introduces* can *and* can't *for talking about abilities in statements, yes/no questions, and short answers*

3 Grammar Focus: *Fluency practice with* can *and* can't *and* too *and* either

4 Pronunciation: *Contrasts the pronunciation of* can *and* can't

WORKBOOK: Exercises 1–3 on pages 37 and 38

Cycle 2

5 Conversation: *Introduces the expressions* be good at *and* know how to

6 Word Power: *A vocabulary-building exercise on sports that practices* know how to

7 Grammar Focus: *Fluency practice with* be good at *and* know how to

8 Listening: *Practices distinguishing between* can *and* do *by choosing the grammatically correct response to a question*

9 Reading: *Amazing facts about the abilities of animals*

Interchange 10: *A fluency activity that reviews* can *and* can't *and talking about abilities*

WORKBOOK: Exercises 4–6 on pages 39 and 40

1 SNAPSHOT

SB p. 62 This activity introduces the theme of sports.

■ Books closed. Write the following chart on the board:

OLYMPIC SPORTS	
Winter games	Summer games

Have students call out the names of sports for the winter and summer games; write them in the chart.

■ Ask: "What country has the most gold medals for downhill skiing? What country has the most gold medals for free-style swimming?" Students call out their guesses.

■ Books open. Students read the Snapshot silently and then compare their answers with the information in the text.

■ Model the names of the sports; students repeat. Then read the three discussion questions with the class. Students write answers individually.

■ When students have finished, they share answers either in small groups or as a class.

Optional activity

■ Work as a class to come up with as many sports as possible. Students call out all the sports they can; write these on the board to form a class list. Which of these are Olympic sports? (5 minutes)

2 CONVERSATION

SB p. 62 This conversation presents *can* and *can't* for talking about abilities.

■ Books open. Students cover the text. Look at the picture of Katherine and Philip. Ask: "What season is it? What are Katherine and Philip wearing? What do you think Katherine and Philip are talking about?"

■ Books closed. On the board write: "Can Katherine swim?" Play the tape and then have students answer as a class. (Answer: "Yes, she can.")

■ Books open. Play the tape again; students listen and read.

■ Present the conversation line by line; students repeat. Explain or demonstrate the difference between "I can't dive at all" and "I can't dive well."

■ Students practice the conversation in pairs using the Look Up and Say technique.

■ If you wish, have several pairs act out their conversation for the class.

3 GRAMMAR FOCUS: *can* with abilities

SB pp. 63 and 64 This Grammar Focus practices *can* and *can't*.

> **Grammar note**
>
> In this unit, *can* is used to talk about abilities. It is not necessary to discuss other meanings of *can* at this stage.

■ Books open. Play the tape or model the language in the box. Students listen and repeat.

1

■ Have students look at the pictures. Then play the tape. Students listen and write *can* or *can't*.

(instructions continue on next page)

■ Alternatively, you can have students complete the sentences according to the illustrations and then listen to the tape to check their answers.

■ If you wish, have students compare answers in pairs before you go over the answers with the class. Play the tape a final time so that students can confirm their answers, if necessary.

■ Pairs take turns saying the sentences.

Tape transcript with answers

1 Katherine is talking about what she can and can't do. Listen and practice.

a) I <u>can</u> draw.
b) I <u>can</u> write poetry.
c) I <u>can</u> fix a car.
d) I <u>can</u> play the piano.
e) I <u>can't</u> sing very well.
f) I <u>can't</u> cook very well.

2 Pair work

■ Explain the task: Students complete the sentences in part 1 with answers that are true for them.

■ Model the sample conversation with *too* and *either*. Then pairs compare information and talk about their abilities.

■ Bring the class back together and ask several students around the room to share their answers with the class.

3 Group work

■ Explain the task and model the sample language. Identify each of the activities in the pictures as a class.

■ Students do the task in groups of four or five. When one student answers a question, that same student asks someone else a question so that everyone has a turn to ask and answer. Students write their classmates' names and check off the things they can do. (They do not write anything if the classmate *can't* do an activity.)

■ Bring the class back together. Ask one student from each group to report to the class about one or more of the activities. For example: "Keiko and Tai-lin can dance. Ana can't dance. I can't dance, either."

4 PRONUNCIATION: *can* and *can't* 🔲

SB p. 64 This activity contrasts *can*, which is reduced in complete sentences, with *can't*, which is never reduced.

> **Pronunciation note**
>
> Because the final *t* in *can't* is not pronounced strongly, students sometimes think they are hearing *can*. This activity helps students hear the difference. *Can't* /kænt/ is never reduced. *Can* is reduced to /kən/ in full sentences. In short answers, however, *can* is not reduced. For example, in the Grammar Box on page 63, *can* is reduced in the first two columns, but not in the last one:
>
> /kən/ /kən/
> I *can* swim. *Can* I swim?
>
> /kæn/ /kæn/
> Yes, I *can*. / I *can* (too).
>
> It is not necessary to explain this to students at this time, unless they reduce *can* inappropriately.

1

■ Books open. Play the tape or model the sentence with *can* and *can't*. Students repeat and practice.

2 Pair work

■ Explain the task: Students work in pairs and take turns saying one of the sentences. Their partner decides whether it is a sentence with *can* or *can't*.

■ If you wish, after the pair work, do the task as a class to check everyone's comprehension.

Extra practice

■ Students practice the Conversation in exercise 2 again, this time paying attention to the reduced vowel in *can* and the full vowel in *can't*.

5 CONVERSATION

SB p. 64 This conversation introduces the expressions *be good at* something and *know how to* do something. It also introduces more vocabulary for sports and abilities.

- Books closed. Say: "Matthew is asking Philip about his new girlfriend. What languages can she speak? Listen."

- Play the tape; students listen for the answer. Then ask the class to respond as a group. (Answer: She can speak Spanish and Japanese.) Ask selected students what else Katherine can do. (Answer: She can play tennis and basketball.)

- Books open. Play the tape again; students listen and read.

- Present the conversation line by line; students repeat. Provide an additional example of the meaning of *be good at* and *know how to* by telling the class about some abilities of your own.

- Students practice the conversation in pairs.

- If you wish, have pairs substitute Katherine's information with information about a friend. Then they practice the conversation again.

6 WORD POWER: Sports

SB p. 65 This activity presents vocabulary for various sports.

1

- Books open. Play the tape as students listen and read.

- Play the tape again. This time students listen and repeat. Then students practice the sentences chorally and individually.

2

- Explain the task: Students work individually to divide the activities into team and individual sports. Then they add two more sports to each list. (Alternatively, this task can be done in pairs.)

- Students compare their work with a partner or other pair before you go over the answers with the class.

- Ask several students to call out the additional sports they listed. Write these on the board to form a class list.

Answers

Team sports	*Individual sports*
basketball	golf
baseball	tennis
football	Ping-Pong
soccer	
volleyball	

3 Pair work

- Explain the task and model the sample conversation. Then pairs take turns asking and answering.

- Bring the class back together and ask several pairs to share a question and answer with the class.

7 GRAMMAR FOCUS:
be good at; know how to

SB p. 66 This Grammar Focus practices *be good at* and *know how to* by talking about activities and abilities.

Grammar notes

1. If it seems appropriate, point out that *be good at* is followed by a plural countable noun (e.g., "sports") or a singular uncountable noun (e.g., "math"), whereas *know how to* is followed by the base form of a verb.

2. Although *be good at* is followed by a noun or noun phrase in the examples in this activity, it can also be followed by a gerund, as in the Conversation on page 64: "She's not good at remembering things." *Know how to*, on the other hand, can never be followed by a gerund. It is only followed by the base form of a verb. It is not necessary to explain this at this point unless students have specific questions.

■ Books open. Play the tape or model the language in the box. Students listen and read.

■ Play the tape or model the language again. Students repeat.

1   Pair work

■ Read the list of questions with the class. Use the photos to explain vocabulary as necessary.

■ Students work alone to write five additional questions. Circulate to help with vocabulary.

■ Students take turns asking and answering the questions in pairs.

2

■ Lead students through the example sentence. Then have them work individually to write five similar sentences about their partner in part 1.

■ Bring the class back together and have several students read one or more of their sentences to the class.

Optional activity: *You're hired!*

■ *Preparation* Write job titles on pieces of paper and hand them out to the class. Students pretend they are employers who are going to hire someone to do the job. They write several questions. For example, for the title "ski instructor" students might write:

Are you good at skiing?
Do you know how to teach?
Do you like cold weather?

Possible job titles: soccer coach; basketball/soccer (etc.) player; language teacher; sports announcer (on radio or TV); sports reporter (for a newspaper); musician (for a restaurant or night club); lifeguard at a pool.

■ *Role play* When students have written their questions, they work in pairs. Student A is the employer first; A asks B questions, and B answers with his or her own information. At the end of the "interview," A says "You're hired!" or "Sorry, you're not hired."

■ Then they switch roles, and Student B is the employer. (10 minutes)

---

8 LISTENING

SB p. 66 This activity practices listening for the auxiliary verb in a question and choosing a grammatically correct response.

■ Books open. Explain the task and have students read the possible responses.

■ Play the tape two or three times. Students choose the grammatically correct response for each question as they listen.

■ Have students compare their answers with a partner. Then go over the answers with the class.

Tape transcript

Listen to questions and choose the best response.

a) We play soccer every Sunday afternoon, and we need another person for the team. Do you know how to play soccer?

b) There's an exciting party on Saturday, and I can't dance very well. Can you teach me how to dance this week?

c) I'm not very good at math. Can you help me with my algebra?

d) There's a barbecue at my house on Friday night, and I need some help. Do you know how to cook steaks?

e) Let's play a game of cards. I love bridge. Do you know how to play bridge?

f) Excuse me. I have this letter from my boyfriend, and I can't understand it. Can you read Italian?

Answers

a) No, I don't.   c) Yes, I can.   e) No, I don't
b) Yes, I can.   d) Yes, I do.   f) No, I can't.

Optional activity

■ Play the recording again. Have students identify the problem each speaker has. [*Note:* In (e) the problem is less clear: The person wants to play bridge and can't play alone.]

---

9 READING 🔊

SB p. 67 This activity practices reading for detail in three short paragraphs about animals.

■ Books open. Students look at the photos. Ask what the animals are and what they know about them. If necessary, use the photos to define the animal names.

1

■ Students read the three paragraphs silently and fill in the chart. If you wish, introduce the paragraphs by playing the tape as students read.

■ Tell students that there may not be an answer in the paragraphs for every space on the chart (see Answers below).

■ Have students compare their answers with a partner. Then go over them with the class.

Answers

Kangaroo
Can: travel 40 miles an hour; jump (20 feet at a time, over a car)
Can't: walk

Camel
Can: live without water for a week; live without food for a long time; walk over 200 miles without water
Can't: (the paragraph does not say what the camel can't do)

Chimpanzee
Can: use sign language
Can't: always use correct grammar

2

■ Explain the task and go over the example with the class. Students work individually to write an interesting fact about an animal.

■ If students have difficulty thinking of interesting things about animals, provide them with some prompts to work with. For example:

	Can	*Can't*
dogs	guard homes	climb a tree
cats	see well at night	fly
ants	carry heavy things	run

■ Bring the class back together, and have several students read a sentence to the class.

INTERCHANGE 10:
Hidden talents

`SB p. IC-13` This class activity reviews and
practices *can* and *can't*.

1 Class activity

■ Books open to page IC-13. Explain the task and
model the sample conversation.

■ Read the list of question prompts with the class
and elicit meanings of any unfamiliar vocabulary.
Three of the new expressions are illustrated.
Students may need help with "touch your toes,"
"musical instrument," "tango," "underwater,"
and "hands."

■ Students stand and mingle to ask each other
questions and write down the names of the people
who *can* and *can't* do the things listed.

2

■ When things begin to quiet down, bring the
class back together. Model the sample language,
and then have several students report some of
their results to the class.

Optional activity

■ Form groups of four or five students who do not
often work together. Students first work alone to
write one sentence about what they think each of
the other students can do. They use *can, is good
at*, or *knows how to*. For example: "I think Carlos
can play the piano well. I think Kyoko is good at
team sports. I think Roxanna knows how to fix a
car."

■ Students take turns reading a sentence. The
others say whether they think the sentence is
true or false. Finally, the person who the sentence
is about tells the group the truth.

A: I think Carlos can play the piano.
B: I think he can play the piano, too.
C: I don't think he can play the piano.
Carlos: Yes, I can.

(10 minutes)

11 When's your birthday?

This unit has two cycles and introduces the topics of birthdays and talking about future plans. It focuses on dates (months and ordinal numbers), talking about the future with *going to*, and future time expressions.

UNIT PLAN

Cycle 1

1 Snapshot: *Introduces the topic of birthdays*

2 Dates: *Presents months and ordinal numbers from* first *to* hundredth

3 Class Survey: *A fluency activity that practices dates by talking about birthdays*

4 Conversation: *Introduces* going to *for talking about the future*

5 Grammar Focus: *Presents new time expressions and practices* going to

6 Pronunciation: *Practices the reduced form of* going to

WORKBOOK: Exercises 1–4 on pages 41 and 42

Cycle 2

7 Listening: *Practices listening for future plans with* going to

8 Celebrations: *A fluency activity that contrasts the present continuous and the future with* going to

Interchange 11: *A fluency activity that reviews the grammar and vocabulary of the unit*

9 Reading: *Practices reading for detail using descriptions of birthday celebrations in the future with* going to

WORKBOOK: Exercises 5–7 on pages 43 and 44

1 SNAPSHOT

SB p. 68 This activity introduces the topic of birthdays by presenting some of the ways people in North America celebrate birthdays.

■ Books closed. Ask students: "What month is your birthday?" Say each month and have students raise their hands. Write the results by month on the board. If necessary, start by going over the names of the months in exercise 2.

■ Then ask: "Are birthdays important (in your culture)? What do people do on their birthdays (in your culture)?" Students can respond simply with one- or two-word answers.

■ Books open. Students read the Snapshot and compare the information to the class poll.

■ Explain the word "ingredients" by referring to the picture on page 59 of the Student's Book (the ingredients of potato salad) or to the reading on page 61 (the ingredients of a hamburger).

■ Use the pictures to illustrate unfamiliar vocabulary. Elicit the meaning of "celebrate."

■ Read the discussion questions with the class. Students answer them individually.

■ Ask students to share their answers with the class. In heterogeneous classes, discuss the differences among various cultures. How important are birthdays in different cultures? How do birthday celebrations compare with those in the U.S.?

Optional activity

■ Groups of four to six students plan the perfect birthday celebration. Who comes? Where does it take place? What do people do? What do people eat and drink?

■ Groups share their plans with the class. The class votes on the best party. (10 minutes)

2 DATES 🔈

SB pp. 68 and 69 This activity presents months of the year and ordinal numbers through hundredth.

1

■ Books open. Play the tape or model the months of the year. Students listen and read.

■ Play the tape or model the months of the year again. This time students listen and repeat.

■ Lead choral and individual practice of the months of the year. Then put students in pairs to say the months back and forth a few times as quickly as possible without looking at the text.

2

■ Play the tape or model the ordinal numbers. Students listen and read.

■ Play the tape or model the numbers again. This time students listen and repeat.

■ Lead choral and individual practice of the numbers.

■ If you wish, students can practice further in pairs. They can take turns saying the numbers, or point to a number in the list and have their partner say it.

■ To practice dates, hold up your book and point to a date on the August calendar in the text. The class says the date. Do this for several dates. Students can practice this further in pairs, with the following variation: One partner says a date; the other points to it on the calendar.

3

■ Model the dates. Then students practice them in pairs.

3 CLASS SURVEY

SB p. 69 This activity practices dates by talking about birthdays.

1

■ Explain the task and model the sample language.

■ Students take out a sheet of paper and make two columns titled "Name" and "Birthday" as in the box.

■ Students move around the classroom, asking classmates when their birthday is and writing the date.

2   Class activity

■ Students compare information. If you wish, ask each student to say the birthday of one classmate. Write this on the board. Then use the class list to find out who has a birthday this week, this month, in the same month, and on the same day.

---

4 CONVERSATION

SB p. 69 This conversation introduces *going to* for talking about the future and expressions for talking about age and birthdays.

■ Books open. Students cover the text. Look at the pictures of Amy and Philip. Ask: "What are they doing?" Students respond simply.

1

■ Play the tape as students listen and read.

■ Present the conversation line by line; students repeat. Explain "embarrassing" by pointing out the expression on Philip's face in the picture. Tell students "I bet" means the same thing as "I think."

■ Students practice the conversation twice in pairs, switching roles so that each student gets a chance to say all the lines.

2

■ Read the instructions and questions as a class. Then students listen to the rest of the conversation and answer the questions. Play the tape several times if necessary.

Tape transcript

2 Listen to the rest of the conversation and answer the questions. a) When is Amy's birthday? How old is she going to be? b) What is she going to do on her birthday?

PHILIP: So when's your birthday, Amy?
AMY: It's in September.
PHILIP: September what?
AMY: September seventeenth.
PHILIP: And are you going to be twenty-one?
AMY: I'm twenty-one now. I'm going to be twenty-two.
PHILIP: Oh. So do you have any plans?
AMY: Well, my birthday is on a Saturday this year, so I'm going to have a party. And of course, I'm going to invite you and Katherine. Can you come?
PHILIP: Well, I think I can. And Katherine can probably come, too.

Answers

a) Amy's birthday is September 17th. She's going to be 22.
b) She's going to have a party on her birthday.

Extra practice

■ Students act out the conversation in part 1 using their own age and birthday instead of Philip's.

5 GRAMMAR FOCUS: Future with *going to* 🔊

SB p. 70 This Grammar Focus practices *going to* for talking about the future, and introduces future time expressions.

> **Grammar note**
>
> *Going to* + verb is used to refer to future plans and intentions. For example, "Are you going to work late?" = "Are you planning to work late?" It thus differs from the use of *go* in the present continuous for describing actions that are happening now (e.g., "I'm going to class right now").

■ Books open. Play the tape or model the language in the boxes. Students listen and read.

■ Play the tape or model the language again. This time, students listen and repeat.

■ To make sure students understand that *going to* has future meaning, ask various students: "What are you going to do after class? What are you going to do next Saturday?"

1

■ Look at the pictures and ask the class to briefly identify the actions. Then ask: "Are you going to do any of these things tonight? Write five things you are going to do tonight, and write five things you are not going to do tonight." Go over the model sentences in the chart.

■ Students do the task individually. *Note:* Students can make up answers rather than give actual information, if they wish.

■ Circulate to help with vocabulary and check for accuracy.

■ Students compare their sentences in pairs. Then ask students to share two sentences with the class.

2 Pair work

■ Explain that students take turns asking about each other's plans for tonight. They can ask about the activities pictured in part 1. They answer with their own information.

■ Students do the task in pairs; after a few minutes, move on to part 3.

3 Pair work

■ Pairs continue the activity, this time asking wh-questions using the time expressions in the box. Model the sample dialogue with a student.

■ When students have finished, ask several pairs to share a question and answer with the class, or ask the questions around the room and have individual students answer.

Optional activity: *The perfect trip*

■ Tell the class to imagine they have won a prize. This summer, they can go anywhere and do anything. Ask: "What are you going to do?"

■ Students work in small groups. Each student tells the others what he or she is going to do.

A: I'm going to go to Paris. I'm going to see the Eiffel Tower.
B: I'm going to go to England. I'm going to meet the queen.
C: I'm going to go to the United States. I'm going to stay at the White House.

■ Bring the class back together; each group shares their most exciting plan with the class. (10 minutes)

6 PRONUNCIATION: *going to* 🔘

SB p. 71 This activity practices the reduced form of *going to*.

> **Pronunciation note**
>
> *Going to* is often reduced to /gənə/ when used to talk about the future in conversational speech. It is not reduced in the present continuous. Compare "I'm going to the store" (cannot be reduced) and "I'm /gənə/ go to the store."

1

■ Books open. Play the tape or model the sentences. Students listen and read.

■ Point out the information in the box and have students listen again.

2

■ Play the tape or model the sentences. Students repeat. Then lead choral and individual practice.

■ Students practice the dialogue in pairs, taking turns being A and B.

Extra practice

■ Students change partners and do the Grammar Focus (ex. 3, part 1) again. This time, students concentrate on using the reduced form of *going to* in their questions and answers. Alternatively, students can practice the Conversation (ex. 4) again using the reduced form of *going to*.

7 LISTENING 🔘

SB p. 71 This activity practices listening for specific information about future plans. The speakers all use the reduced form of *going to*.

1

■ Books open. Read the instructions as a class.

■ Students work alone to imagine what each person is going to do tonight. They write their guesses in the chart.

■ Ask several students to share their guesses with the class. Do not give away the actual plans.

2

■ Set the context: An interviewer on the street is asking people about their evening plans. Students listen to four short interviews.

■ Play the tape. Students listen and write what the people are actually going to do tonight.

■ Have students compare their answers with a partner or in small groups. Then go over them with the class.

Tape transcript

2 Now listen to the people tell about their evening plans. What are they actually going to do?

INTERVIEWER: What's your name?
MICHELLE: It's Michelle.
INTERVIEWER: I bet you're going to go to the gym tonight.
MICHELLE: No, not tonight. I'm going to meet a friend in the park. We're going to run together.

INTERVIEWER: And what's your name?
KEVIN: Kevin.
INTERVIEWER: So are you going home now, Kevin?
KEVIN: Well, no, not right now. First I'm going to go to a video arcade.
INTERVIEWER: Oh, so you're going to play video games.
KEVIN: That's right.

(transcript continues on next page)

INTERVIEWER: Can I ask your name?

ROBERT: Yes, my name is Robert.

INTERVIEWER: Are you going to go anywhere tonight?

ROBERT: Well, there's a party tonight, but I can't go. I'm carrying work home with me. It's right here in my briefcase.

INTERVIEWER: So you're going to work tonight?

ROBERT: Yes, I am.

INTERVIEWER: And what's your name?

JANE: My name is Jane.

INTERVIEWER: Do you have any plans for this evening?

JANE: Do you see this bag? I have some new CDs, so I'm going to listen to some music.

INTERVIEWER: What kind of music is it?

JANE: Jazz. I always listen to jazz.

Sample answers

Michelle: She's going to meet a friend. They're going to run in the park.

Kevin: He's going to play video games.

Robert: He's going to work tonight.

Jane: She's going to listen to some music (jazz).

8 | CELEBRATIONS

SB p. 72 This is a fluency exercise for talking about the future with *going to*.

Pair work

■ As a class, look at each illustration and the sentence below it individually. Make sure that students understand each celebration by asking:

"What is the date of New Year's Eve? What do people do at midnight?"

"What do people do after high school graduation?" (Answer: They get a job or they go to college/university.)

"What is the Fourth of July in the U.S.?" (Answer: It's an important national holiday.)

■ Read the expressions in the box as a class. For each expression, have students demonstrate the meaning with gestures or by pointing out the object or action in the pictures. For the word "kiss," blow a kiss into the air. For the words "diploma" and "fireworks," you may need to draw pictures on the board:

diploma

fireworks

■ Point to the first picture and say: "It's Jeremy's birthday. What are people doing? What's Jeremy going to do?" Write the answers on the board.

■ Working individually, students write at least four sentences about each picture. They write what the people are doing and what they are going to do, using the phrases in the box. (*Note:* Some of these phrases can be used for more than one picture. If you wish, encourage students to use their own phrases in addition to the language provided in the box.)

■ When students have finished, they compare their sentences with a partner.

■ Go over the pictures as a class, and ask individual students to read a sentence.

Alternative presentation

■ Go over each picture as a class, writing a few sample sentences on the board. Then divide the students into groups of four or five and have them write a group "composition" about the picture of their choice. When they are finished, a member from each group can read the composition to the class.

Possible answers

(*Note:* The answers below include all possible choices; students need only write four sentences per picture.)

a) It's Jeremy's birthday. Jeremy is having a party. He and his friends are having a good time. His friends are going to sing "Happy Birthday." Jeremy is going to blow out the candles. He's going to receive some presents. He's going to open the presents.

b) It's New Year's Eve. These people are having a party. They're wearing special hats. They're having a good time. They're going to shout "Happy New Year" at midnight. They're going to kiss their friends.

c) It's Jessica's high school graduation. Jessica and her friends are wearing special hats. They're going to listen to a speech. They're going to receive a diploma. They're going to have a party. They're going to receive presents.

d) It's the Fourth of July in the U.S. These people are having a picnic. They're cooking food on the barbecue. They're having a good time. They're going to watch the fireworks at night.

INTERCHANGE 11:
Vacation plans

SB p. IC-14 This activity practices *going to* by asking and answering questions about vacation plans.

1 Pair work

■ Books open to page IC-14. Explain the task and model the questions in the chart for the class. Ask students to describe some of the pictures, which are intended to give them ideas on how to respond. Give special attention to question (2), "How long . . . ?" and the response, as this is new.

■ Students work individually and answer the questions on the chart.

■ When they have finished, students form pairs. Partners take turns asking and answering the questions. They write down their partner's answers.

2 Group work

■ Pairs join together in small groups. They tell the group about their partner's plans.

■ If you wish, have each group choose the most interesting vacation plan and tell the rest of the class about it.

■ Alternatively, you can take a class poll to see what choices students have made in planning their vacations. You can focus on common destinations, activities, and modes of transportation. Tally the results:

Where?		*What?*	
beach	IIII	swimming	IIII
mountains	II	hiking	III
city	IIII	sightseeing	IIII
country	IIII	reading	JHH
home	I	(etc.)	

9 READING 🔲

SB p. 73 This exercise practices reading for detail.

1

■ Books open. Explain the task: Students read the interviews and then correct the statements.

■ Read the statements as a class first. Then students read the interviews for the correct information.

■ If you wish, play the tape as students read the first time.

■ If students have questions about vocabulary, encourage them to guess the meaning from context. Ask them to guess the meaning of "custom," "life," "surprise," "ceremony," and "opposite."

■ Students compare answers with a partner. Ask them to read the interviews again if they disagree on the correct answer.

■ Go over the answers as a class.

Answers

a) To celebrate her birthday, Elena's friends are going to pull on her ears.
b) Sun Hee's mother is going to cook some noodles on her birthday.
c) On his birthday, Mr. Isai's wife is going to give him something red.
d) Philippe is going to take his friends out to dinner on his birthday.

Optional activity

■ Ask students to make generalizations about the birthday customs in the reading by completing these sentences:

In Spain, when people have a birthday, . . .
In Taiwan, when people have a sixteenth
   birthday, . . .
In Japan, when people have a sixtieth
   birthday, . . .
In France, when people have a birthday . . .

Ask them to tell about any other birthday customs they know.

2

■ Students write several sentences about their next birthday or the birthday of a friend or family member. They can use the paragraphs in the reading as a model.

■ When students have finished, have them exchange paragraphs with a partner. Partners read each other's paragraphs and ask questions if something is not clear.

■ Students revise their paragraphs based on their partner's comments. They can do this in class or for homework. Have them hand in their final versions, or have students read them to the class.

12 What's the matter?

This unit has two cycles and focuses on expressions for talking about health and health problems. It presents and practices vocabulary for illnesses; expressions for making an appointment; imperatives; time expressions with *on, at,* and *in;* and sentence stress.

UNIT PLAN

Cycle 1

1 Snapshot: *Introduces the topic of health*

2 Conversation: *Introduces expressions for talking about health problems*

3 Health Problems: *A vocabulary-building exercise*

4 Listening: *Practices listening for specific information about health problems*

5 Pronunciation: *Practices sentence stress patterns*

WORKBOOK: Exercises 1–2 on pages 45 and 46

Cycle 2

6 Conversation: *Introduces time expressions with* on, at, *and* in, *and imperatives*

7 Time Expressions: *A fluency practice exercise*

8 Grammar Focus: *Practices affirmative and negative imperatives*

9 Reading: *Practices reading for gist and expressing opinions*

Interchange 12: *A fluency activity that reviews the vocabulary of the unit and imperatives*

WORKBOOK: Exercises 3–6 on pages 47 and 48

1 SNAPSHOT

SB p. 74 This activity introduces the topic of health.

■ Books closed. On the board write:

> Common reasons for missing class
> a cold

Students call out (or act out, if they don't know the appropriate word) other reasons why they miss class. Write these on the board.

■ Books open. Students read the Snapshot silently and then compare their answers on the board with the information in the Snapshot.

■ If necessary, go over each of the reasons/problems to make sure students understand the meaning. If you wish, ask how many of the students sometimes have these problems (or how many miss class because of them).

■ Read the discussion questions as a class; then have students answer them in pairs or small groups.

■ Bring the class back together and ask several students to share their answers.

Optional activity

■ Pairs decide which of the reasons presented in the Snapshot are good reasons for missing class and which are not good reasons. Ask the students to rank them from best to worst.

■ Pairs tell the class how they have ranked the reasons. Does everyone agree? (5 minutes)

2 CONVERSATION 📼

SB p. 74 This conversation presents expressions for asking and talking about health problems.

■ Books open. Students cover the text and look at the picture of Brian and Victor. Ask: "What's the matter with Victor? Listen and find out."

■ Play the tape as students listen for the answer to the question. (Answer: Victor is feeling sad.)

■ Play the tape again as students listen and read.

■ Present the conversation line by line; students repeat. Explain that "How are you?" is often a greeting and not a real question. The answer is almost always "fine," or an equivalent expression such as "great," "good," or "not bad." Victor tells Brian he is feeling sad only after Brian asks, "What's the matter?"

■ Have students practice the conversation in pairs. Then ask several pairs to act it out for the class.

3 HEALTH PROBLEMS 📼

SB p. 75 This activity presents vocabulary for parts of the body and practices asking and answering about health problems.

1

■ Books open. Play the tape or model the words as students listen and read.

■ Play the tape again. This time students point to the body part as they hear the instruction "Point to your head," and so on.

Tape transcript

1 Listen. Point to each body part.

Point to your head.
Point to your eyes.
Point to your nose.
Point to your ear.
Point to your mouth.
Point to your teeth.
Point to your neck.
Point to your stomach.
Point to your back.
Point to your shoulder.
Point to your arm.
Point to your hand.
Point to your leg.
Point to your feet.

2

■ Look at the three pictures. Ask the class what's the matter with the person on the right in each picture.

■ Play the tape as students listen and read.

■ Lead choral and individual repetition of the conversations. If you wish, students can practice them in pairs.

■ Ask several pairs to act out one of the conversations for the class.

3   Class activity

■ Read the list of health problems with the class and explain any new vocabulary.

■ Model the sample language and demonstrate the task with a student. Students then take turns acting out an illness for the class. Individual students guess what the illness is by asking yes/no questions. The student who guesses correctly gives sympathy.

4 LISTENING 📼

SB p. 75 This activity practices listening for specific information about health problems.

■ Books open. Explain the task: Students listen to six short conversations about health problems. What body part are the people talking about?

■ Play the tape several times as students do the task.

■ Have students compare answers with a partner or in small groups. Then check answers as a class. If you wish, play the tape a final time so that students can confirm their answers.

Tape transcript

Listen to these people talk about health problems. What's wrong with them? Write the name of the body part where they have a problem.

a)
MAN: I think I'm going to go home early. I don't feel well.
WOMAN: What's the matter?
MAN: I have a sore throat.
WOMAN: Oh, that's too bad.

b)
WOMAN: Are you OK?
MAN: Not really. I have a stomachache.
WOMAN: Why don't you go home?
MAN: Good idea.

c)
MAN: Here, have some ice cream.
WOMAN: I can't eat any cold food.
MAN: Really? Why not?
WOMAN: I have a toothache.

d)
MAN 1: Can you carry my briefcase?
MAN 2: I'm sorry, but I really can't.
MAN 1: Oh. What's the matter?
MAN 2: I have a sore hand.

e)
WOMAN: I'm going to clean the house. Can you help me?
MAN: Well, I can't vacuum. I have a backache.
WOMAN: Maybe you can wash the dishes.
MAN: Well, OK.

f)
MAN: Let's go to a movie tonight.
WOMAN: I don't think I can watch a movie tonight.
MAN: Why not?
WOMAN: I have a terrible headache.
MAN: OK, so let's go home.

Answers

a) throat	c) tooth/teeth	e) back
b) stomach	d) hand	f) head

5 PRONUNCIATION: Sentence stress 🔊

SB p. 76 This activity develops an awareness of a stress pattern in English.

> **Pronunciation note**
>
> Each sentence in this activity has a word that receives greater stress than the other words in the sentence. The word is generally a "content" word that appears toward the end of the sentence. This word also receives the highest pitch. (Although many sentences have more than one important word that receives stress, it is not necessary to explain this to students at this time.)

1

■ Play the tape or model the sentences as students listen and read. Point out the word in each sentence that gets the most stress.

■ Play the tape again; students repeat. Lead choral repetition of the sentences again to practice.

2 Class activity

■ Explain the task: Students listen to the conversation and underline the syllable with the most stress in each sentence.

■ Play the tape several times as students do the task.

■ Students compare answers in pairs and then share answers as a class. Play the tape a final time if necessary.

■ Students practice the conversation in pairs.

Answers

A: What's the <u>prob</u>lem?
B: I have a very high <u>fe</u>ver.
A: Are you taking some <u>as</u>pirin?
B: Yes, I <u>am</u>. And I'm drinking a lot of <u>wa</u>ter.

6 CONVERSATION 🔊

SB p. 76 This exercise introduces the use of *on*, *at*, and *in* with time expressions, as well as imperatives.

■ Books open. Students cover the text and look at the picture of Susan and the receptionist (top right). Ask: "What do you think Susan is doing?" (Answer: She's calling the doctor's office.) Look at the other picture (bottom) and ask: "What's the matter with Susan?" Students guess the answer. Do not say if they are correct.

■ Play the tape as students listen to find out what is wrong with Susan. Then ask the class to answer. (She has a backache.)

■ Play the tape again as students listen and read.

■ Present the conversation line by line; students repeat. Elicit the meanings of "make an appointment," "sit down," "pills," and "every four hours." Give special attention to the expression "don't lift heavy things."

■ Students practice the conversation in groups of three. They may act out the conversation three times, switching roles each time.

■ If you wish, ask some groups to act out the conversation for the class.

7 TIME EXPRESSIONS:
on, at, and *in* 🔘

SB p. 77 This activity practices using *on, at,* and *in* with time expressions.

■ Books open. Play the tape or model the language in the box. Students listen and repeat.

■ If you wish, randomly read the nouns only from the box and have the class respond with the appropriate preposition. For example:

T: June.
Ss: In June.

Pair work

■ Students work individually to complete the conversations with *on, at,* or *in* as appropriate.

■ Check answers as a class by calling on pairs of students to read each conversation aloud. Ask students to guess the meaning of "holiday," "opening," and "I have trouble remembering things" from context.

■ Students practice the conversations in pairs. If you wish, have pairs perform a conversation for the rest of the class.

Answers

A: Are you free on Sunday? There's a party at Victoria's place.
B: Is the party in the afternoon?
A: No, it starts at 8:00 P.M.
B: But I never go to parties on Sunday nights. I go to work at 7:30 A.M. Monday.
A: But the party is on July 3rd. You don't work on the Fourth of July. It's a holiday.

A: Can I make an appointment in June? I'm free on Wednesdays.
B: Can you come on Wednesday the 7th?
A: On the 7th, I can only come in the morning.
B: I have an opening at ten in the morning.
A: Good. So the appointment is on Wednesday the 7th at 10:00 A.M.
B: That's right. See you then.

A: Can I have an appointment on Tuesday the 6th?
B: In the morning?
A: No, in the afternoon, please.
B: Can you come at three o'clock?
A: That's fine. So my appointment is at three o'clock on the 13th.
B: Well, no, it's on Tuesday the 6th. By the way, what's your problem?
A: I have trouble remembering things. When is my appointment again?

8 GRAMMAR FOCUS:
Imperatives 🔘

SB p. 78 This activity presents affirmative and negative imperative statements.

■ Books open. Play the tape or model the sentences in the box as students listen and repeat.

1

■ Read the sentences in the box as a class. Explain that students must match each sentence to an appropriate picture.

■ Have students do the task individually; then go over the answers with the class.

Answers

a) I have a stomachache.
b) There's no food in the house.
c) I can't sleep at night.
d) I have a headache.
e) My job is very stressful.
f) I have a fever.
g) I can't lose weight.

(instructions continue on next page)

2 Pair work

■ Explain the task: Students give advice to the people in part 1. They can choose from the advice in their book or they can make up their own advice. Note that "aspirin" does not usually add -*s* for the plural.

■ Read the advice as a class.

■ Students do the task in pairs. They take turns pretending to be the person in the picture while their partner gives advice. Encourage them to use gestures in presenting their problem. Students can make up their own problems if they wish.

■ Ask pairs to share a problem and advice with the class.

9 READING 🔲

SB p. 79 This exercise asks students to react to an article by giving their own opinions on health.

■ Books open. Look at the picture of the Delany sisters. Ask: "How old are they?" Students guess, and then scan the reading for the answer.

1

■ Students read the article. If you wish, play the tape as they read.

■ Students do the task individually.

■ Students compare answers in pairs or small groups. Then ask several students to share one or more of their answers with the class.

2

■ Students work individually to write five pieces of advice for living a long life. Circulate to help with vocabulary.

■ Students form groups and read their advice to each other. Each group chooses the best advice and reads it to the class.

Optional activity: *A short life*

■ Students write five sentences giving "advice" on how to live a short life. For example: "Smoke a lot of cigarettes. Eat a lot of fat."

■ Students call out their worst piece of advice. (10 minutes)

INTERCHANGE 12: Helpful advice

SB p. IC-15 This fluency activity gives additional practice with imperatives and reviews the vocabulary of the unit.

■ Books open to page IC-15. Look at the pictures and the speech bubbles as a class.

1 Pair work

■ Students work in pairs. They read each problem and then give several pieces of advice. If you wish, ask pairs to give three pieces of advice to each person.

■ When you have finished, bring the class back together and share the advice that pairs gave in each instance.

Alternative presentation

■ If you wish, when pairs have given their advice for each person, have them write their advice in random order on the board. Then the class decides which person the advice is for.

2 Class activity

■ Students write down two problems that they have. (If they are embarrassed to do this, tell everyone to make up their problems.)

■ Students take turns telling the class their problems. The other students call out advice. Alternatively, go around the class and have each student give advice, until no one can think of anything else to advise.

Review of Units 9–12

This unit reviews the vocabulary of food and health, names of months and ordinal numbers, *can* and *can't* to talk about abilities, and *going to* for the future.

UNIT PLAN

1 Mealtime: *Reviews adverbs of frequency and food vocabulary*

2 Your Favorite Fruit: *A fluency activity about food*

3 Listening: *Reviews the topics of health, food, and abilities, and practices listening in order to make inferences*

4 Abilities: *Reviews* can *and* can't, know how to, *and* be good at

5 Important Dates: *A fluency activity that reviews months, ordinal numbers for dates, and* going to *for future plans*

6 Weekend Plans: *Reviews* going to *for future plans*

7 Listening: *Reviews the vocabulary of food and shopping and practices choosing appropriate responses to spoken questions*

1 MEALTIME

`SB p. 80` This activity reviews adverbs of frequency and the vocabulary of food.

Pair work

■ Books open. Explain the task and lead students through the information in the box.

■ Students work individually to complete the chart with the things they eat for breakfast, lunch, and dinner.

■ Students take turns asking and answering the questions in pairs, for example:

"What time do you usually eat breakfast?"
  "I usually eat breakfast at 7:00 A.M."
"Where do you usually eat breakfast?"
  "I usually eat breakfast at home."
(etc.)

■ Bring the class back together and ask several pairs to share a question and answer with the class.

2 YOUR FAVORITE FRUIT

`SB p. 80` In this activity, students review food vocabulary.

Pair work

■ Books open. Demonstrate the task: Think of a fruit and have the class ask you the list of questions in the book. Answer the questions and ask the class to guess what fruit you are thinking of.

■ Students do the task in pairs. They take turns thinking of a fruit.

■ Bring the class back together, and ask a few students to describe their favorite fruit to the class. The class guesses what it is.

3 LISTENING: What's the matter? 🔲

SB p. 80 This activity practices listening and making inferences, and reviews the topics of health, food, and abilities.

■ Books open. Read the list of problems with the class. Explain that students will hear six short conversations. They match the conversation to the problem.

■ Play the tape several times as students do the task.

■ Ask students to compare their answers with a partner. Then play the tape again as students check and revise their work.

■ Go over the answers with the class.

Tape transcript

Listen to these conversations. Match the conversation to the problem.

a)
A: Hi, how are you?
B: Oh, not too good.
A: What's the matter? Are you sick?
B: No, I'm fine. I guess I feel a little blue.

b)
A: This hamburger isn't very good.
B: Really? What's wrong with it?
A: I don't know. It needs something.
B: Well, it has mayonnaise, pickle, and onion on it.
A: Yeah, but something is wrong.

c)
A: How do you feel?
B: Terrible. I have a headache and my whole body feels sore.
A: Do you have a fever?
B: I think so.
A: Go home early and go to bed.
B: Good idea.

d)
A: Are you going to go to Angela's party?
B: No, I don't think so.
A: Why not? It's going to be fun.
B: Well, there going to be music, and everyone is going to dance. And I'm not very good at that.

e)
A: How do you feel today?
B: Oh, about the same.
A: Can I carry your briefcase for you? I bet it's heavy.
B: Thank you so much. I can't really carry heavy things.

f)
A: What are you doing? Are you getting up?
B: Yes, I am. I can't sleep.
A: What are you going to do?
B: I think I'm going to read my lecture notes again. I can't remember anything!

Answers

a) 4   b) 1   c) 6   d) 3   e) 2   f) 5

4 ABILITIES

SB p. 81 This activity reviews using *can* to ask and answer questions about abilities.

■ Books open. Explain the task and read the list of items with the class.

■ Students work individually to write four sentences about their abilities.

■ Model the sample questions with the class. Also model a few questions with *know how to* and *be good at*: "Do you know how to play chess?" "Yes, I do." "Are you good at tennis?" "Yes, I am."

■ Students then work in pairs to guess their partner's abilities. Remind students that *can* is reduced in full sentences, both questions and statements.

5 IMPORTANT DATES

SB p. 81 This activity practices months and ordinal numbers for dates, as well as *going to* for future plans.

Pair work

■ Books open. Explain the task and model the example. The holidays and celebrations can be from the students' own cultures.

■ Pairs take turns talking about what they are going to do on four future holidays or celebrations.

■ Bring the class back together and have several students tell the class what they are going to do on one of the dates.

6 WEEKEND PLANS

SB p. 81 This activity offers further review of *going to* in wh-questions and statements.

Pair work

■ Books open. Explain the task and lead students through the chart.

■ Students complete the chart individually with their own plans. If they do not have any specific weekend plans, encourage them to come up with some tentative plans.

■ Model the sample language. Then students work in pairs and take turns asking and answering questions about each other's weekend plans.

■ Bring the class back together and ask several students what they are going to do over the weekend.

7 LISTENING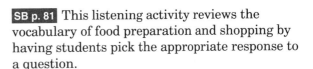

SB p. 81 This listening activity reviews the vocabulary of food preparation and shopping by having students pick the appropriate response to a question.

■ Books open. Explain the task: Students are going to hear six different questions. Read the possible responses as a class.

■ Play the tape as students choose the best response for each question.

■ Students compare answers with a partner. Then play the tape again and have students check and revise their work.

■ Go over the answers with the class.

Tape transcript

Some people are getting ready for a barbecue. Listen to the questions. Choose the best response.

a) I think there are going to be twelve people at the barbecue. Oh, wait, are Helen and Bob going to come?

b) I'm going to go shopping this afternoon. Can we make a shopping list?

c) What do we need for the barbecue? Do we need any soda?

d) Let's serve some potato salad. Do you know how to make it?

e) By the way, we need ketchup for the hamburgers. Do we have any?

f) What's your favorite dessert? Do you like strawberries and ice cream?

Answers

a) No, they have the flu.
b) Yes, but we need some paper.
c) Yes, buy some.
d) No, I don't.
e) No, we need some.
f) No, I like chocolate cake.

13 Can you help me, please?

This unit has two cycles and introduces language for asking and giving directions. It focuses on vocabulary for common places in a city or town, the pronunciation of compound nouns, prepositions of place, and giving directions using the imperative.

UNIT PLAN

Cycle 1

1 Word Power: *A vocabulary-building exercise for common places in a city or town*

2 Pronunciation: *Practices word stress in compound nouns*

3 Conversation: *Introduces prepositions of place for describing location in a city or town*

4 Listening: *Practices listening for specific information about places around town and what they sell*

5 Grammar Focus: *Practices prepositions of place*

6 Listening: *Practices listening for prepositions of place to make inferences about a destination*

WORKBOOK: Exercises 1–3 on pages 49 to 51

Cycle 2

7 Conversation: *Introduces the imperative in giving directions*

8 Snapshot: *Presents facts about tourist attractions in New York City*

9 Directions: *Practices the imperative for giving directions*

10 Reading: *Practices reading directions and reading for specific information*

Interchange 13: *Fluency practice with the grammar and vocabulary of the unit*

WORKBOOK: Exercises 4–5 on pages 51 and 52

1 WORD POWER 📼

SB pp. 82 and 83 This activity introduces vocabulary for common places around town.

1

■ Books open. Look at the pictures and say the words under each one. Then explain the task. Do (a) as a class. Ask: "Where can you buy books?"

■ Students do the task individually.

■ Play the tape so that students can check their answers.

■ Go over the answers with the class.

■ Play the tape again. This time students listen and practice the sentences.

Tape transcript

a) You can buy books at a bookstore.
b) You can buy a fish dinner at a restaurant.
c) You can buy carrots at a supermarket.
d) You can buy stamps at a post office.
e) You can buy a television at a department store.
f) You can buy gasoline at a gas station.
g) You can buy aspirin at a drugstore.
h) You can buy a magazine at a newsstand.

Answers

b) 4   d) 8   f) 7   h) 3
c) 1   e) 6   g) 2

2   Pair work

■ Explain the task and read the questions with the class.

■ Pairs take turns asking and answering the questions. Then bring the class back together, and ask the questions around the class.

■ For extra practice, students write three more questions to add to the list. Then pairs join together in groups of four to ask and answer questions.

Optional activity

■ Write these questions about places in your city or town on the board:

Name three restaurants in (name of your town).
Name two places where you can buy a notebook.
Where can you buy a stereo?
Where can you have fun?

■ Small groups answer the questions and then add three more questions to the list.

■ Bring the class back together; groups share their answers and questions with the class. (10 minutes)

2 PRONUNCIATION: Compound nouns 📼

SB p. 83 This activity practices the pronunciation of compound nouns.

1

■ Books open. Explain that a compound noun is a word made up of two nouns. Some are written as two words (e.g., post office), others as a single word (e.g., drugstore). The greatest stress is usually on the first part of the compound noun (e.g., **post** office, **drug**store).

■ Use the tape to demonstrate the stress in each of the words. Students listen and practice.

2

■ Students look through the Word Power (ex. 1) to find four more compound nouns and write them in the blanks.

■ Call on students to read some of the words from their lists. Ask them to pay attention to word stress.

■ If you wish, ask students to review Unit 2 (or another unit) and find more compound nouns to practice. Here are some examples from Unit 2 (in alphabetical order):

book bag	**dri**ver's license	**hand**bag
briefcase	**eye**glasses	**news**paper
credit cards	**hair**brush	**sun**glasses

3 CONVERSATION 🔘

SB p. 83 This conversation presents expressions for describing location using prepositions of place.

■ Books open. Students cover the text and look at the picture. Ask: "Who do you think these people are? What do you think they are saying?"

■ Books closed. Write this question on the board: "What is the boy's problem?" Then play the tape as students listen for the answer. Ask students to answer as a group. (Answer: The boy needs a bathroom.)

■ Books open. Play the tape as students listen and read.

■ Present the conversation line by line; students repeat. Explain that "I'm sorry, but I don't think so" is a polite way of saying "no." See if students can figure out the meaning of "restroom" from the context. Point out that the word "restroom" is used mainly for public buildings and "bathroom" for houses and apartments.

■ Students practice the conversation in pairs. Then, if you wish, have several pairs act out the conversation for the class.

4 LISTENING 🔘

SB p. 83 This activity practices listening for specific information about what people are going to buy and where they are going to shop.

■ Books open. Explain that students will hear four short conversations about people who are going to buy something. Read the chart as a class.

■ Play the tape several times as students fill in the chart.

■ Students compare answers with a partner. Then play the tape again and have students check their work before going over the answers with the class.

Tape transcript

What are these people going to buy? Where are they going to buy it? Listen and complete the chart.

a) Sarah
KUMIKO: Hey, Sarah. Are you going to go to the beach with us on Sunday?
SARAH: I think so, but I have a problem.
KUMIKO: What's the matter?
SARAH: I need a bathing suit. So I'm going to go shopping downtown this afternoon. I'm going to a department store.
KUMIKO: Can I come with you?
SARAH: Sure. You can help me.

b) Michael
NICOLE: Hi, Michael. Are you going to go to the gym tonight?
MICHAEL: No, not tonight. I'm going to go to the supermarket.
NICOLE: To the supermarket?
MICHAEL: I'm going to cook dinner tomorrow evening, and I need some chicken.
NICOLE: Oh. Do you know how to cook?
MICHAEL: Yeah, I'm pretty good at it.

c) Jennifer
DAVID: Hi, Jennifer. How are you?
JENNIFER: Oh, not great. I have a terrible headache.
DAVID: That's too bad.
JENNIFER: And I don't have any aspirin. Do you have any?
DAVID: No, I don't. Sorry.
JENNIFER: Then I think I'm going to go to the drugstore and buy some.

d) Victor
BRIAN: Let's go to a movie tonight. What do you think, Victor?
VICTOR: Good idea, but which movie?
BRIAN: Hm. I don't know.
VICTOR: We need a newspaper. Is there a newsstand near here?
BRIAN: There's one on Third Street.
VICTOR: OK. See you in a minute.

Answers

		What	*Where*
a)	*Sarah*	bathing suit	department store
b)	*Michael*	chicken	supermarket
c)	*Jennifer*	aspirin	drugstore
d)	*Victor*	newspaper	newsstand

5 GRAMMAR FOCUS: Prepositions of place 🔊

SB pp. 84 and 85 This activity presents and practices prepositions of place.

Note: The prepositions of place need to be visualized and memorized, and the best way to do this is to use the visual information supplied by the map to reinforce learning. (Of course, students will remember some of these expressions from Unit 2, ex. 9.)

■ Books open. Give students a minute or two to look at the map. Then play the tape or model the sentences in the box. Students listen and read.

■ Play the tape again. This time students point to the places on the map as they hear the sentences.

■ If students need more practice, name places on the map (e.g., "hotel") and ask students to say where the places are in as many ways as possible.

1

■ Explain the task. Students work alone to complete the sentences.

■ Ask students to compare their answers with a partner or in a small group. Then go over them with the class.

Answers

a) There's a bus stop <u>in front of</u> the department store.
b) There's a parking lot <u>near</u> the department store.
c) The parking lot is <u>behind</u> the Grand Hotel.
d) There's a gas station <u>next to</u> the parking lot.
e) There's a restaurant <u>on</u> Grant Street, <u>between</u> Third and Fourth Streets.
f) The restaurant is <u>between</u> a drugstore and a bookstore.
g) The bookstore is <u>on the corner</u> of Grant and Fourth.

2 Pair work

■ Explain the task: Students use the map on page 84 to complete the conversations with the correct prepositions of place. They do the task individually.

■ Have students compare answers with a partner. Then go over them with the class by calling on pairs of students to read the conversations aloud.

■ Pairs practice the conversations. If you wish, have a few pairs act out one of the conversations for the class.

Answers

A: Excuse me, sir. Is there a restaurant <u>near</u> here?
B: Well, there's a new restaurant <u>on</u> Grant Street. It's <u>across from</u> Kelly's Supermarket. But it's expensive.
A: Isn't there a coffee shop <u>on</u> Third Street?
B: Yes, it's <u>on the corner of</u> Lincoln and Third.

A: Excuse me, miss. Is there a gas station <u>on</u> Washington Street?
B: Yes, there is. It's <u>on the corner of</u> Washington and Second.
A: So it's <u>behind</u> the Grand Hotel.
B: Right. And it's <u>next to</u> a big parking lot.

3 Pair work

■ Explain the task and model the sample conversation. Then pairs take turns asking and answering questions about places in their neighborhood.

Optional activity

■ Students draw a simple map of the area around their home and write their name on the paper. Then students exchange maps around the room. Pairs take turns asking and answering about the map they received, like this:

A: Is there a bookstore near Tom's house?
B: Yes, there is. It's on . . .

(10 minutes)

6 LISTENING 🔊

SB p. 85 This activity practices listening for specific information about a destination and making inferences about the destination.

■ Books open. Explain that students are going to hear three short conversations giving directions to places on the map on page 84.

■ Play the tape as students look at the map and write the name of the place where each person is going. If necessary, play each conversation several times before moving to the next one.

■ Ask students to compare their answers with a partner or in a small group. Then play the tape again so that students can check their work.

■ Go over the answers with the class.

Tape transcript

Look at the map on page 84 as you listen to these conversations. Where are these people going?

a)
MAN: Hm. I think it's on Grant Street.
WOMAN: Is it near Kelly's Supermarket?
MAN: Yes, it is. It's right across from Kelly's.
WOMAN: Oh, yeah. There's a drugstore there.
MAN: Right. It's between the drugstore and a bookstore.

b)
WOMAN: Is it near Newman's Department Store?
MAN: Yes, it is. There's a hotel right across from Newman's.
WOMAN: The Grand Hotel?
MAN: Right. It's behind the hotel there. It's next to a gas station.
WOMAN: OK. Thank you very much.

c)
WOMAN: Is it near the post office?
MAN: Well, it's on the same street – it's on Fourth Street.
WOMAN: On the corner of Fourth and Grant?
MAN: No, it's on the corner of Fourth and Washington.
WOMAN: OK. Thanks.

Answers

a) restaurant   b) parking lot   c) City Bank

7 CONVERSATION 🔊

SB p. 85 This conversation presents expressions for asking for and giving directions.

■ Books open. Students cover the text and look at the picture. Ask: "Where do you think these people are? What is this building?" Students guess, but do not reveal the correct answers.

■ Play the tape as students listen and read. Ask the two questions again, and have students answer. (Answers: They're in New York City. This is the Empire State Building.)

■ Present the conversation line by line; students repeat. Explain that "How do I get to . . . " is a way of asking for directions. Point out the two meanings of "right," as in "on the right" and "right behind you." "Right" = "exactly" in the second case. Use actions to demonstrate "turn around" and "look up."

■ Students practice the conversation in pairs, changing roles after the first time. If you wish, ask a few pairs to act out the conversation for the class, using appropriate gestures.

8 SNAPSHOT

SB p. 86 This activity presents information about tourist attractions in New York City.

■ Books closed. Ask: "Do you want to visit New York City? What can you see there?" As students call out places they know about, write them on the board.

■ Books open. Ask pairs of students to choose one tourist attraction and try to understand the information given below it. Circulate to help students with unfamiliar vocabulary.

■ Students answer the discussion questions in pairs or small groups. Then ask groups to share their answers with the class.

9 DIRECTIONS 🔲

SB p. 86 This activity presents language for giving directions. Students practice with a map of New York City.

- Books open. Play the tape or model the sentences. Students listen and read.

- Play the tape or model the sentences again. This time students repeat and practice.

- Explain the task: Students silently read the three sets of directions. They use the map to find out where the directions lead. They circle the building or mark it with (a), (b), or (c).

- Ask students to compare their answers with a partner. Then go over them with the class.

Answers

a) the Museum of Modern Art
b) the New York Public Library
c) the Empire State Building

Optional activity

- Students work in pairs to write a set of directions from the Empire State Building to a different building on the map. Then pairs exchange papers and follow the directions they receive to find out where they lead. (10 minutes)

10 READING 🔲

SB p. 87 This activity practices reading for specific information.

- Books open. Play the tape as students listen and follow the directions on the map on page 86.

1

- Explain the task. Students read the text and follow the directions on the map on page 86.

- If you wish, play the tape as students read. Alternatively, play the tape in part 2 as students read the text a second time in order to answer the questions.

2

- Read the questions with the class. Then have students read the text again to find the answers.

- Ask students to compare their answers with a partner or in small groups. Then go over them with the class.

Answers

a) Empire State Building
b) Rockefeller Center
c) Bryant Park
d) St. Patrick's Cathedral

3

- Explain the task and go over the example. Then have students work individually to write two sentences about their town for each question.

- Circulate to help with vocabulary and check for accuracy.

- Ask several students to read one or more of their sentences to the class.

INTERCHANGE 13: Directions

SB pp. IC-16 and IC-18 This information-gap activity gives additional practice in asking for and giving directions.

Pair work

▪ Divide the class into pairs and assign each student the role of Student A or Student B.

▪ Student A's turn to page IC-16 and Student B's turn to page IC-18. Tell partners that they should not look at each other's pages.

1

▪ Explain the task: Student A asks Student B how to find a car wash, a supermarket, and a flower shop. Student B gives directions, and A follows them on the map. Student A writes the name of the store on the appropriate building.

▪ Model the sample language and example. Then students do the task in pairs.

2

▪ Students change roles. Now Student B asks Student A how to find a coffee shop, a shoe store, and a bookstore.

▪ When talk begins to die down, bring the class back together. Ask several pairs to ask for and give directions to one of the places.

Optional activity

▪ Bring in a map of the city or town where your school is located. Students ask for and give directions to places on the map. (10 minutes)

14 Did you have a good weekend?

This unit has two cycles and introduces the simple past tense through talking about weekend activities. It presents the past tense of regular and irregular verbs, pronunciation of regular past tense verbs, and vocabulary for leisure activities.

UNIT PLAN

Cycle 1

1 Snapshot: *Introduces the topic of weekend activities*

2 Word Power: *Builds vocabulary for weekend activities through a word map*

3 Conversation: *Introduces the past tense of regular verbs*

4 Grammar Focus: *Presents affirmative and negative statements in the past tense with regular verbs*

5 Pronunciation: *Presents pronunciation of past tense ending -ed*

WORKBOOK: Exercises 1–3 on pages 53 and 54

Cycle 2

6 Conversation: *Introduces questions and statements in the past tense with irregular verbs*

7 Grammar Focus: *Presents the past tense forms of irregular verbs*

Interchange 14: *A fluency activity that practices the past tense forms of regular and irregular verbs*

8 Listening: *Practices listening for the gist of conversations about past events*

9 Reading: *Practices reading a history of the weekend for specific information*

WORKBOOK: Exercises 4–7 on pages 55 and 56

1 SNAPSHOT

SB p. 88 This activity introduces the topic of leisure activities by presenting information about how people in the United States spend their weekends.

■ Books closed. Ask students: "What do you do on the weekend?" Students call out answers as you write them on the board.

■ Books open. Students read the information in the Snapshot and then compare the activities in the Snapshot with those they have listed.

■ Students answer the discussion question individually. Then they compare answers in small groups or as a class.

■ If you wish, ask all of the students to call out the amount of time they spend on the activities in the Snapshot. Create a class list on the board. Then calculate class averages and see if your list agrees with the Snapshot.

2 WORD POWER

SB p. 88 This word-map activity builds vocabulary for weekend activities.

■ Books open. Explain the task and read the list of words and examples with the class.

■ Students work individually to add the activities to the word map. Then they add two more activities of their own to each category.

■ Write the four categories on the board. Students call out the activities from the list. Then have students come up to the board and write their additional words.

Answers

(*Note:* Some activities can go into more than one column. For example, reading can be either relaxation or entertainment. Encourage students to explain their answers simply.)

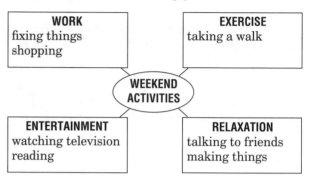

3 CONVERSATION 🔲

SB p. 89 This exercise introduces the past tense of regular verbs in the context of talking about weekend activities.

■ Books open. Have student cover the text and look at the picture. Say: "This is Michael and this is Nicole. Who relaxed on the weekend?" Students guess and call out their answer.

■ Play the tape as students listen and read.

■ Present the conversation line by line; students repeat. Explain that "I bet" means "I think" and that "sort of" means "to a degree" and is used when an answer is neither "yes" nor "no."

■ Students practice the conversation in pairs at least twice, changing roles. If you wish, have several pairs act out the conversation for the class.

4 GRAMMAR FOCUS: Past tense of regular verbs 🔊

SB pp. 89 and 90 This activity presents the past tense form of regular verbs.

> **Grammar note**
>
> The simple past tense is used for actions that were begun and completed in the past. The auxiliary verb *did* (the past of *do*) is used to form negative statements in the past tense and is followed by the base (simple) form of the main verb.

- Books open. Play the tape or model the language in the box. Students listen and read. Point out that *didn't = did not*.

- Play the tape again. This time students listen and repeat.

- Point out the words in the spelling box and play the tape. To see if students can figure out the spelling rules, ask them to spell the past tense of these regular verbs:

wash (washed)   carry (carried)
dance (danced)   stay (stayed)

If you wish, explain the spelling rules.

> **Spelling note**
>
> To form the past tense of regular verbs, you usually add *-ed*. If the verb ends in *e*, just add *-d*. If the verb ends in a consonant + *y*, drop the *y* and add *-ied*.

1

- Explain the task: Students talk about the Conversation in exercise 3. They talk about what Nicole and Michael did and didn't do, using the activities in the box. Model the sample language.

- Students silently read the Conversation again. Then pairs talk about Nicole's and Michael's weekend activities.

- Bring the class back together and ask several students to say one thing Nicole or Michael did or didn't do.

2 Pair work

- Look at the pictures and model the words. Then go over the example sentences in the chart.

- Students work individually to write five things they did and five things they didn't do last weekend.

- Model the sample language below the box. Then students take turns telling a partner about their weekend.

- Bring the class back together and ask each student to tell the class one thing he or she did or didn't do.

Optional activity: *What did you do last night?*

- Students work individually to write two false statements and one true statement about the things they did and didn't do last night.

- Bring the class back together and have students take turns reading their statements. The class guesses which statement is true. (10 minutes)

5 PRONUNCIATION: Past tense 🔲

SB p. 90 This activity practices the three different ways of pronouncing the regular past tense.

> **Pronunciation note**
>
> The rules for pronouncing the regular past tense are as follows:
>
> 1. Use /d/ if the verb ends in a vowel or voiced consonant (except /d/).
> 2. Use /t/ if the verb ends in a voiceless consonant (except /t/).
> 3. Use /ɪd/ if the verb ends in /d/ or /t/.
>
> This information is mainly for the teacher. The most important thing for students to know is when to add the extra syllable /ɪd/.

1

■ Books open. Play the tape or model the verbs as students listen and read.

■ Play the tape again as students listen and practice.

2

■ Play the tape or model the verbs once or twice. Students listen and write the verbs in the appropriate list.

■ Have students compare their answers with a partner or in a small group. Then play the tape or model the verbs again so that students can check their answers.

■ Go over the answers with the class.

Answers

/t/	/d/	/ɪd/
fixed	opened	started
missed	listened	attended
walked	loved	skated
asked		hated
washed		

■ If students need extra practice, have them work in pairs: Students take turns saying one of the verbs. Partners point to the verb they hear.

6 CONVERSATION 🔲

SB p. 91 This exercise introduces the past tense form of irregular verbs.

■ Books open. Students cover the text and look at the picture. Say: "Stephanie and Laura are talking about Stephanie's date with Richard. Listen. What did they do?"

■ Books closed. Play the tape. Students listen for what Stephanie and Richard did. Then ask the class to answer. (Answer: They went to a movie, *Police Partners II,* and they went to a dance club.)

■ Books open. Play the tape again as students listen and read.

■ Present the conversation line by line; students repeat. Ask the class: "Stephanie didn't like the movie. Why did Stephanie tell Richard she liked it?" (Answer: She wanted to be polite/nice).

■ Students practice the conversation in pairs.

■ If you wish, have several pairs act out the conversation for the class.

7 GRAMMAR FOCUS: Past tense of irregular verbs 🔲

SB pp. 91 and 92 This activity presents and practices the past tense forms of 33 common irregular verbs.

> **Grammar notes**
>
> 1. Point out that students will have to memorize the past tense forms of irregular verbs.
>
> 2. The auxiliary verb *do* is used in past tense yes/no questions and wh-questions. *Do* is the past tense marker (*did*); the main verb stays in base form (or simple form). For example, "*Did* you *eat* lunch?"

■ Books open. Play the tape or model the sentences in the box on the left. Students listen and read. Then play the tape again as students listen and repeat.

1

- Students individually complete the chart on the right with the present tense form of the verbs.

- Ask students to compare answers with a partner or in a small group. Then go over the answers with the class. If necessary, model each of the tense forms and have students repeat.

Answers

Present	Past	Present	Past
blow	blew	put	put
buy	bought	read	read
come	came	run	ran
do	did	say	said
draw	drew	see	saw
drink	drank	sing	sang
drive	drove	sit	sat
eat	ate	sleep	slept
feel	felt	stand	stood
find	found	swim	swam
get	got	take	took
give	gave	teach	taught
go	went	tell	told
have	had	think	thought
know	knew	wear	wore
make	made	write	wrote
meet	met		

2   Pair work

- Students work individually to fill in the blanks in the conversations with the correct verb forms.

- Have students compare answers with a partner. Then go over the answers with the class.

- Students practice the conversations in pairs twice, switching roles.

A: Did you have a good weekend?
B: Yes, I did. I had a great weekend.

A: Did you go to a restaurant last night?
B: No, I didn't. I ate dinner at home.

A: Did you read the newspaper this morning?
B: Yes, I did. I read the newspaper before work.

A: Did you have/eat breakfast this morning?
B: Yes, I did. I had toast and tea.

3   Pair work

- Explain the task and read the list of questions with the class. Then students silently choose seven of the questions to ask a partner.

- Model the sample conversation. Then pairs take turns asking and answering the questions they chose.

- Bring the class back together and have several pairs share a question and answer with the class.

INTERCHANGE 14:
Past and present

SB p. IC-17 This fluency activity gives students more practice asking and answering past tense questions.

1   Pair work

- Books open to page IC-17. Explain the task and model the sample conversation. Then read the list of question prompts with the class and explain any unfamiliar vocabulary by using the illustrations.

- Students take turns asking and answering the questions in pairs. They write down their partner's answers.

2   Group work

- Explain the task and model the sample language.

- Two pairs join together to form a small group. Then students take turns telling the group about their partner.

- Bring the class back together, and have several students tell the class one interesting thing about their partner as a child and now.

8 LISTENING 🔲

SB p. 92 This activity practices listening for specific information given in the past tense.

■ Explain the task: Students listen to four short conversations. What did each man do on Saturday morning? They match the name to the picture.

■ Look at the four names and the four pictures. Ask the class what the person is doing in each picture.

■ Play the tape as students do the task. Repeat as necessary.

■ Students compare their answers with a partner or in a small group. Then play the tape again and have students check their answers.

■ Go over the answers with the class.

Tape transcript

Listen to four men talk about their weekends. What did they do on Saturday morning? Write the names under the pictures.

AMY: Hey, Matthew. Did you go to the beach on Saturday?
MATTHEW: No, I didn't. I got up too late. I slept until noon. I always sleep in on the weekends.

KATHERINE: I called you on Saturday morning, Philip. But there was no answer.
PHILIP: Oh? Well, I – I left the house early. I went to the swimming pool.
KATHERINE: Oh, so you got a little exercise.
PHILIP: Yeah, I did. I can't swim very well, of course, but I'm good at diving.

LINDA: So, Chris, did you do anything interesting last weekend?
CHRIS: Well, I went shopping for some clothes.
LINDA: Oh, did you buy anything?
CHRIS: No, I didn't. Everything is so expensive these days.

LAURA: Hi, Mark, how are you?
MARK: Fine, really great.
LAURA: Did you have a good weekend?
MARK: Yeah, on Saturday morning I read a great book.
LAURA: What book was it?
MARK: A really interesting book on Central America.

Answers

(in order from left to right)
Mark Matthew
Philip Chris

9 READING 🔲

SB p. 93 This activity practices reading for gist in an article that gives the history of the weekend.

■ Books open. Explain the task and read the sentence halves at the bottom of the page with the class. Encourage students to predict the answers.

■ Students read the text silently and then work individually to match the sentence halves. (*Note:* Students should be able to do the task without understanding every word of the reading.)

■ Students compare their answers with a partner. If necessary, students reread the text. This time, if you wish, play the tape as students read.

■ Go over the answers with the class.

■ If you wish, pick some terms from the reading, such as "holy day" and "blue Mondays," and discuss their meaning. See if students can figure out the definitions from the context.

Answers

a) Before 1800, [3] people generally rested and prayed on Sundays.
b) In the early 1800s, workers [5] didn't rest on Sundays, and then felt too tired to work on Mondays.
c) In 1874, English workers [4] stopped work at one o'clock on Saturdays.
d) By 1930, American workers [2] began to take off Saturday afternoons.
e) After 1940, American workers [1] had a two-day weekend.

15 Where were you born?

This unit has two cycles and practices talking about personal history. It introduces dates with years, expressions for talking about birthplace, questions and statements with *was* and *were,* negative contractions, and wh-questions with *did, was,* and *were.*

UNIT PLAN

Cycle 1

1 Snapshot: *Introduces the topic of birthplace*

2 Conversation: *Introduces dates with years and sentences with* was *and* were

3 Years: *A fluency activity*

4 Listening: *Practices listening for birthplace and birth date*

5 Grammar Focus: *Practices statements and questions with* was *and* were

6 Pronunciation: *Practices negative contractions*

WORKBOOK: Exercises 1–3 on pages 57 and 58

Cycle 2

7 Conversation: *Introduces wh-questions with* did, was, *and* were *and more expressions for giving personal history*

8 Grammar Focus: *Practices wh-questions and answers in the past tense*

Interchange 15: *A fluency activity that reviews the grammar and vocabulary of the unit*

9 Reading: *Practices reading for gist and for specific information in short biographies of famous people*

WORKBOOK: Exercises 4–7 on pages 59 and 60

1 SNAPSHOT

`SB p. 94` This activity introduces the topic of birthplace by presenting information about three famous Americans born in other countries.

■ Books closed. Write the names "Albert Einstein," "I. M. Pei," and "Martina Navratilova" on the board. Ask if students know who they are. Then say: "These famous Americans were not born in the United States. Where do you think each person was born? Guess the country."

■ Students write down their guesses.

■ Ask several students for their predictions, but do not say whether they are right or wrong. If students aren't familiar with these names, skip this part of the procedure.

■ Books open. Students read the information in the Snapshot and check their predictions.

■ Ask questions around the class, such as "What does I. M. Pei do? Where was Albert Einstein born?"

■ Read the discussion question to the class. Students write their answers and then compare with a partner or in a small group.

■ Bring the class back together and ask several students to share their answers with the class.

2 CONVERSATION

`SB p. 94` This activity introduces years and statements and questions with *was* and *were* in a conversation about personal history.

■ Books open. Have students look at the picture of Melissa and Chuck. Ask the students to guess the topic of conversation: "What do you think they are talking about?"

■ Play the tape as students listen and read. Check to see if any students correctly predicted the topic of conversation.

■ Present the conversation line by line; students repeat.

■ Work with the pronunciation of "1992." See if students can guess the meaning of "right away," "wow," and "fluent" from the context.

■ Students practice the conversation in pairs two times, changing roles the second time.

3 YEARS

`SB p. 95` This activity presents years and provides practice using the information from the conversation in exercise 2.

1

■ Books open. Have students look over the years listed. Then play the tape or model the years. Students listen and read.

■ Play the tape or model the years again. Students listen and repeat.

■ Working in pairs, students take turns saying a year. Partners point to the year they hear.

2

■ Explain the task: Students look at the pictures of Melissa and then answer the questions.

■ Read the questions with the class. Then pairs take turns asking and answering the questions.

Optional activity: *When was that?*

■ Write on the board five questions about past events that students are likely to know about. For example:

> *When did World War II start? (1939)*
> *When did it end? (1945)*
> *When was (famous person) born?*
> *When did (country) win the World Cup soccer*
>   *tournament? (or other popular sport)*
> *When did (name) become prime minister*
>   *(president, etc.) of (your country)?*

■ Students write their answers and then compare them in pairs or small groups.

4 LISTENING 🔊

SB p. 95 This activity practices listening for specific information about when and where three famous people were born.

■ Books open. Explain the task: Students listen to three short conversations about these people. They listen for their place of birth and birth date.

■ Look at the pictures. Encourage students to predict the answers.

■ Play the tape as students do the task. Students check to see if their predictions were correct. Repeat the tape as necessary.

■ Students compare answers with a partner. Then play the tape again so that students can check their work.

■ Go over the answers with the class.

Tape transcript

Where were these people born? When were they born? Listen and complete the chart.

WOMAN: You know, I read an interesting article on Elizabeth Taylor yesterday.
MAN: Really?
WOMAN: Yeah. Did you know that she was born in England?
MAN: No, I didn't.
WOMAN: Yeah, she was born in London in nineteen thirty-two.
MAN: In nineteen thirty-two? Wow, she looks great for her age.
WOMAN: Yeah, she really does.

MAN: I'm going to see that new Michael J. Fox movie tonight.
WOMAN: Michael J. Fox? Was he in *Back to the Future*?
MAN: Yes, he was. By the way, did you know that he was born in Canada?
WOMAN: Really? I thought he was American.
MAN: Well, he was born in Alberta, Canada, in nineteen sixty-one.
WOMAN: In nineteen sixty-one? But he looks so young.

MAN: Is Mel Gibson Australian?
WOMAN: I don't know. Let's check this book on movie stars. It says here that he was born in New York, but that he moved to Australia when he was twelve.
MAN: But he was born in the United States. By the way, how old is he?
WOMAN: Well, he was born in nineteen fifty-six. How old does that make him?

Answers

	Elizabeth Taylor	*Michael J. Fox*	*Mel Gibson*
Place of birth	(London) England	(Alberta) Canada	(New York) United States
Year of birth	1932	1961	1956

5 GRAMMAR FOCUS: Statements and questions with *was* and *were* 🔊

SB p. 96 This activity presents and practices statements and questions with *was* and *were*.

■ Books open. Play the tape or model the language in the boxes. Students listen and read.

■ Play the tape or model the language again. This time students listen and repeat.

■ If you wish, practice by asking students questions that will likely produce both negative and affirmative answers: "Were you born in (name of country)?" They answer: "Yes, I was" or "No, I wasn't." Then make sentences about the students like this: "Juan and Kumiko weren't born in . . . They were born in . . . "

1

■ Students work alone to fill in the blanks in the conversations with the correct verb forms. Then they compare answers with a partner.

(instructions continue on next page)

■ Check answers as a class. Then have students practice the conversations in pairs.

Answers

A: Where were you born?
B: I was born in Brazil.
A: Were your parents born there, too?
B: Yes, they were. They were born in Rio.

A: When was your daughter born?
B: She was born in 1990.
A: How old were you then?
B: I was twenty-five.

A: How was your weekend?
B: It was OK.
A: Was the weather nice?
B: No, it wasn't. It rained every day.

2 Pair work

■ Students complete the questions individually with *was* or *were.*

■ Go over the answers with the class.

■ Students work in pairs. They take turns asking and answering the questions with their own information, as in the sample dialogue.

■ When talk begins to die down, bring the class back together and ask several pairs to share their most interesting question and answer.

Answers

a) Were you born in this city?
b) When were you born?
c) Were your parents born here?
d) When was your mother born?
e) When was your father born?
f) Were you a good student in high school?
g) What was your favorite subject?
h) Were you good at sports?
i) Were you good at languages?
j) Who was your first English teacher?

Extra practice

■ Pairs write three similar questions to add to the list. Then two pairs join together to ask and answer questions. (5 minutes)

6 PRONUNCIATION: Negative contractions

SB p. 97 This activity practices the pronunciation of various negative contractions.

1

■ Books open. Play the tape or model the contractions. Students listen and read.

■ Play the tape again. Students listen and practice.

2

■ Model the sentences. Students listen and repeat.

■ Lead choral and individual practice. Then have pairs take turns saying the sentences back and forth.

7 CONVERSATION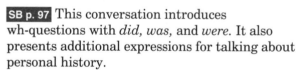

SB p. 97 This conversation introduces wh-questions with *did, was,* and *were.* It also presents additional expressions for talking about personal history.

■ Books open. Students cover the text and look at the pictures of Chuck and Melissa. Explain that this conversation continues the conversation in exercise 2. Say: "Now Melissa is asking Chuck about his life. When did Chuck come to Los Angeles? Listen and find out."

■ Books closed. Play the tape. Ask what year Chuck came to Los Angeles. (Answer: 1978) Students answer chorally.

■ Books open. Play the tape again as students listen and read.

■ Present the conversation line by line; students repeat. If necessary, explain or mime the words "major," "drama," and "actor."

■ Students practice in pairs.

■ If you wish, have a few pairs act out the conversation for the class.

8] GRAMMAR FOCUS:
Wh-questions with *did,*
was, and *were* 🔊

SB p. 98 This activity presents wh-questions with
did, was, and *were.*

> **Grammar note**
>
> Notice the different formulas for making
> questions with *did* versus *was/were:*
>
> (Wh-word) (*was/were*) (noun/pronoun) (complements)
>   What   was   your major   in college?
>
> (Wh-word) (*did*) (noun/pronoun) (main verb)
>   When   did   you   come . . . ?
>
> The main verb in questions with *did* is in the
> base form, or simple form.

■ Books open. Play the tape or model the
language in the box. Students listen and read.

■ Play the tape again. Students listen and repeat.

■ Practice the sentences in the grammar box.
Either ask a question and have the class answer
chorally, or have the left side of the class ask the
question and the right side of the class answer.
Alternatively, students can practice in pairs.

What's the question?

■ Explain the task and go over the example.
Students work individually to write the
appropriate questions for each response.

■ Have students compare their work with a
partner. Then go over the correct questions with
the class.

■ If you wish, have pairs take turns asking and
answering the questions.

Answers

b) Where were you born?
c) Where did you grow up?
d) Where did you go to high school?
e) Who was your best friend in high school?
f) What was your favorite course in high school?
g) How old were you when you entered college?
h) What was your major in college?
i) Why did you choose history?

Extra practice

■ Pairs of students ask each other the questions
they wrote for the Grammar Focus. They answer
with their own information. Question (i) should
be based on the answer to question (h).

INTERCHANGE 15: Timeline

SB p. IC-20 This activity gives students additional
practice with years; asking and answering
wh-questions with *was, were,* and *did;* and
talking about personal history.

1 Pair work

■ Books open to page IC-20. Explain the task and
go over the example.

■ Students work individually to write five
important events from their life and to mark the
dates on the timeline.

■ Circulate to help with vocabulary.

2

■ Explain the task: Students tell each other the
five years they have marked on the timeline.
Their partner asks what happened in each year
and then asks further questions about the event.
Model the sample language with a student.

■ Students do the task in pairs, asking and
answering questions about the five important
years. They write down their partner's answers.
The answers can be in note form – they do not
have to be complete sentences.

■ Bring the class back together, and have
students tell the class about one important event
in their partner's life. In large classes, this step
may be done in groups.

9 READING 🔲

SB p. 99 In this activity students read short biographies of famous people, first for gist and then for specific information.

1

■ Books open. Explain the task and go over the four names. Ask the class if they know anything about the people. Students call out anything they know.

■ Students read the text and match the names to the paragraphs. If you wish, play the tape as students read.

■ Go over the answers with the class.

Answers

a) Leonardo da Vinci
b) Amelia Earhart
c) Walt Disney
d) Neil Armstrong

2

■ Explain the task: Students read again to complete the chart. Encourage students to guess from context the meaning of the expressions "stolen," "solo transatlantic flight," "disappeared," "animated cartoon character," and "stepped." *Note:* The date column refers to the year in which that person did something important.

■ Students compare answers with a partner or in a small group. Then go over the answers with the class.

Answers

Name: Walt Disney
Profession: artist and film producer
One important thing: created Mickey Mouse
Date: 1928

Name: Leonardo da Vinci
Profession: painter
One important thing: painted the *Mona Lisa* (the most famous painting in the world)
Date: about 1504

Name: Amelia Earhart
Profession: aviator
One important thing: completed a solo flight across the Atlantic (also acceptable: first woman to fly across the Atlantic as a passenger in 1928)
Date: 1932

Name: Neil Armstrong
Profession: astronaut
One important thing: first person to walk on the moon
Date: July 20, 1969

3

■ Explain the task. Students work individually to write a few sentences about a famous person from their country. The sentences can form short paragraphs.

■ Circulate to help with vocabulary and check for accuracy.

■ Students read their paragraphs to each other in small groups or to the class.

■ Students can use the other students' criticisms and comments to help them revise their work. The revision can be done as an in-class or a homework assignment.

Alternative presentation

■ Students read their descriptions to the class without mentioning the name of the famous person. The class guesses who the person is.

16 Hello. Is Jennifer there, please?

This unit has two cycles and focuses on the functions of making telephone calls, making invitations, and giving excuses. It practices additional expressions with prepositions of place, the use of subject and object pronouns, the form verb + *to* + verb (e.g., *have to go*), and pronunciation of the reduced forms of *want to* and *have to*.

UNIT PLAN

Cycle 1

1 Snapshot: *Introduces the topic of telecommunications*

2 Conversation: *Introduces new uses for prepositions of place, expressions for talking on the telephone, and subject and object pronouns*

3 Places: *Practices prepositions of place*

4 Grammar Focus: *Practices subject and object pronouns*

WORKBOOK: Exercises 1–3 on pages 61 and 62

Cycle 2

5 Conversation: *Introduces expressions for making invitations and excuses, and the form verb + to + verb*

6 Grammar Focus: *Practices affirmative and negative sentences with the form verb + to + verb*

7 Pronunciation: *Practices the reduced forms of* want to *and* have to

8 Excuses: *A fluency activity on the grammar of this cycle that practices the function of making excuses*

Interchange 16: *An information-gap activity that practices the vocabulary and grammar of the unit through invitations and excuses*

9 Listening: *Practices listening to telephone messages for gist and specific information*

10 Reading: *Practices reading articles about activities for specific information*

WORKBOOK: Exercises 4–6 on pages 63 and 64

1 SNAPSHOT

SB p. 100 This activity introduces the topic of home telecommunications.

■ Books closed. Tell students: "One of the ways we can communicate with friends is by telephone. What are some other ways?" Ask pairs to list all of the ways that people can stay in touch with each other.

■ Pairs call out their answers.

■ Books open. Students read the Snapshot and compare their list with the information presented.

■ Model the words and read the discussion questions with the class.

■ Students silently write answers to the questions. Then they compare answers around the class or in small groups.

2 CONVERSATION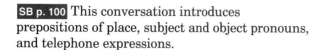

SB p. 100 This conversation introduces prepositions of place, subject and object pronouns, and telephone expressions.

1

■ Books open. Look at the picture. Say: "Michael and Tracy are talking on the phone."

■ Play the tape as students listen and read.

■ Present the conversation line by line; students repeat. Explain that "complicated" = "difficult" and that "pal" = "friend."

■ Students practice the conversation in pairs. Then, if you wish, have a few pairs act out the conversation for the class.

2

■ Explain the task: Students listen to the message Michael leaves on the answering machine. They write down why Michael called Jennifer.

■ Play the tape two or three times as necessary as students do the task.

■ Ask students to compare their answer with a partner. Then go over the answer with the class.

Tape transcript

2 Now listen to Michael's message. Why did he call Jennifer?

[recording on an answering machine]
JENNIFER: Hi, this is Jennifer.
TRACY: And this is Tracy.
JENNIFER: We can't come to the phone right now, so please leave your name and phone number after the beep. We'll call you back as soon as we can. [*beep*]

MICHAEL: Hi, Jennifer. This is Michael. Michael Lynch. There's a great movie at the Odeon Theater on Thursday. It's the new Spielberg film. Uh, I can't remember the name of it, but it's really good. Anyway, do you want to go? There's a show at eight P.M. and it finishes at ten. If you want to go, call me at 555-2871. Talk to you soon.

Answer

Michael wanted to invite Jennifer to a movie.

3 PLACES 📼

SB p. 101 This activity presents the prepositions of place *at*, *in*, and *on* in relation to location of people (e.g., she's *at* work; he's *in* the yard).

1

■ Books open. Play the tape or model the language. Students listen and read. Then repeat the tape as they listen and practice.

2 Pair work

■ Explain the task and model the sample conversation.

■ Pairs take turns calling and answering about the six people. (*Hint:* The expressions for describing where the people are, and thus why they can't come to the phone, are all listed in part 1 of this exercise.)

■ Bring the class back together, and have several pairs act out one of the conversations for the class.

Answers

Michael: He's in the shower.
Lisa: She's at the pool.
Brian: He's on the roof.
Sarah: She's at class.
Victor: He's at work.
Nicole: She's in the hospital.

4 GRAMMAR FOCUS: Subject and object pronouns 📼

SB p. 102 This activity presents and practices subject and object pronouns.

> **Grammar note**
>
> Make sure that students know what a subject and object are. Every sentence has a subject. For example, in the sentence "**Michael** left a message," "Michael" is the subject. The subject performs an action. "Michael" can be replaced with a subject pronoun: "**He** left a message."
>
> Now look at this sentence: "Michael left **Jennifer** a message." "Jennifer" is an object and can be replaced with an object pronoun: "He left **her** a message." Object pronouns can be "direct" objects, "indirect" objects," or objects of prepositions.

■ Books open. Play the tape or model the language in the box. Students listen and repeat.

■ Ask students to point out the subject and object pronouns in the examples. Mention that *it* and *you* have the same subject and object forms.

Pair work

■ Students work individually to complete the conversations with the correct subject or object pronoun. If they have trouble, you may have them do the task in pairs, or start the exercise as a class.

■ Check answers as a class. Then students practice the conversations in pairs.

Answers

A: Is Robert there, please?
B: I'm sorry, he's not here right now. Do you want to leave him a message?
A: Yes, this is David. Please tell him to call me at work.
B: Can you tell me your phone number there?
A: Sure, it's 555-2981.

(answers continue on next page)

A: Can I speak with Mr. Ford, please?
B: He's not in today. But maybe I can help you.
A: Can you tell him to call John Rivers?
B: John Rivers. OK. Does he have your number?
A: Yes, I'm sure he has it.

A: This is the answering machine for Tom and Bill. Please leave us a message after the tone.
B: Bill, this is Maria. You left your hat and gloves here yesterday. If you need them, come and pick them up this evening. Hey, I love your hat. Where did you buy it?

5 CONVERSATION 🔲

SB p. 102 This conversation introduces questions and statements with verb + *to* + verb (e.g., *want to go, have to stay*) and gives expressions for making invitations and giving excuses.

■ Books open. Look at the picture of Michael and Jennifer and set the scene: Jennifer is calling Michael back. This continues the story from the Conversation in exercise 2, in which Michael asked Jennifer to go to a movie.

■ Play the tape as students listen and read.

■ Present the conversation line by line; students repeat.

■ Students practice the conversation in pairs.

Extra practice

■ Pairs practice the conversation again, substituting a different invitation and excuse.

■ Ask a few pairs to act out their conversation for the class.

6 GRAMMAR FOCUS:
Verb + *to* + verb 🔲

SB p. 103 This activity presents questions and statements with verb + *to* + verb.

> **Grammar note**
>
> It is not necessary at this stage to provide students with a complete grammatical explanation of this form. Rather, simply explain that *to* can be used to join two verbs. The second verb is always a base form and thus never changes. For example:
>
> I **want** to **go**.
> I **wanted** to **go**.
> He **wants** to **go**.

■ Books open. Play the tape or model the language in the box. Students listen and read. Then play the tape again; students practice.

■ For further practice, say the affirmative form of each of the sentences in the grammar box. Students respond with the negative form. Then switch roles: You say the negative form and they say the affirmative. For example:

T: I want to go to the movies.
Ss: I don't want to go to the movies. (etc.)

1

■ Explain the task: Students silently complete the conversations with *have to, need to, like to,* or *want to* as appropriate.

■ Check answers as a class.

■ Students practice the conversations in pairs. Ask a few pairs to do one of the conversations for the class.

Answers

A: This is a beautiful hat. I want to buy it.
B: Please don't buy it. We need to save money.

A: I love Chinese, and I want to speak it fluently.
B: Then you have to/need to study very hard. It's a difficult language.

A: Do you want to go dancing tonight?
B: I really want to go, but I can't. I have to work late.

A: I don't have to/don't need to work this Saturday, so let's go to the beach.
B: That sounds great. But we have to/need to clean the house first.

A: Do you want to go to a party next Friday?
B: Thanks, but I don't like to go to parties.

2   Pair work

■ Explain the task and read the list of questions with the class.

■ Students silently write answers to the questions.

■ Pairs take turns asking and answering the questions. Then ask several pairs to share one or more answers with the class.

7   PRONUNCIATION: *want to, have to* 🔊

SB p. 103 This activity practices pronunciation of the reduced forms of *want to* and *have to*.

Note: Point out to students that these are spoken forms and not written forms.

1

■ Books open. Play the tape or model the sentences. Students listen and read. Then play the tape again as students listen and practice.

■ Lead choral and individual practice of the sentences. If necessary, lead repetition of /wanə/ and /hæftə/.

2   Pair work

■ Students practice the conversations in the Grammar Focus (ex. 6) again, this time concentrating on the pronunciation of the reduced forms of *have to* and *want to*.

8   EXCUSES

SB p. 104 This activity gives additional practice with the verb forms presented in exercise 6.

1   Pair work

■ Books open. Explain the task and read the list of excuses with the class.

■ Students work individually and decide how often they use these excuses.

■ Students compare their responses with a partner. Which three excuses do they use the most?

■ Ask several students to call out their favorite excuse.

2   Class activity

■ Explain the task: Students write down three places they want to go and when they want to go there.

■ Model the sample conversation. Students turn down the invitation the first time and give an excuse; the second time the invitation is offered they accept it.

■ Students mix and mingle to invite at least three classmates to go with them.

Optional activity

■ Students write three "silly" excuses in pairs, for example: "I have to wash my dog" or "I want to stay home and clip my nails."

■ Bring the class back together and have pairs read their excuses aloud.

■ The class votes on the "silliest" excuse. (5–10 minutes)

INTERCHANGE 16:
Let's make a date

`SB pp. IC-19 and IC-21` This information-gap activity gives students additional practice with invitations and excuses in a communicative context.

■ Put students in pairs and assign each the role of either Student A or Student B.

■ Student A's turn to page IC-19 and Student B's turn to page IC-21. They should not look at each other's pages.

1

■ Explain the task and model the sample conversation. Student A invites B, and B replies, giving an excuse if B is not available. Then B picks another date and asks A. They continue back and forth until they find a date when they are both free.

2

■ Explain the task and model the sample conversation. Pairs decide what they are going to do on their date.

■ Bring the class back together and ask each pair to tell the class what they are going to do and when they are going to do it.

9 LISTENING 🔲

`SB p. 104` This activity practices both listening for gist and listening for detail in telephone answering machine messages.

1

■ Books open. Explain the task: Students will hear five separate telephone answering machine messages left by different people. Read the list of names with the class. Students check who can and who can't come.

■ Play the tape once or twice as students do the task.

■ Compare answers around the class.

Tape transcript

1 Jennifer invited friends to a party on Saturday. Listen to the messages on her answering machine. Who can come? Who can't come?

[recording on an answering machine]
JENNIFER: Hi, this is Jennifer.
TRACY: And this is Tracy.
JENNIFER: We can't come to the phone right now, so please leave your name and phone number after the beep. We'll call you back as soon as we can. *[beep]*

KUMIKO: Hello, Jennifer? This is Kumiko. Thanks for the invitation. I'd love to come. So, see you on Saturday at around eight o'clock. *[beep]*

DAVID: Hey, Jennifer. This is David. I'd like to come to your party, but I have to go out to dinner with my parents. It's my mother's fiftieth birthday, so it's sort of important. I'm really sorry. Talk to you soon. *[beep]*

SARAH: Hi, Jennifer. This is Sarah calling. Thanks for inviting me to your party. I'm going to be a little late. I hope that's OK. Can I bring some food or soda? Call me at 555-3806. *[beep]*

VICTOR: Hi, Jennifer. This is Victor. Thanks for inviting me to your party on Saturday. I'd love to come. I'm going to bring some chips and soda. I hope that's OK with you. If not, call me. You know my number. Bye. *[beep]*

NICOLE: Hi, Jennifer. This is Nicole. I'm really sorry, but I can't come to your party on Saturday. I'm going to go to a concert with my friend Robert. And I can't change my plans because he has tickets already. Again, I'm really sorry. Talk to you soon.

Answers

	Can come	*Can't come*
Kumiko	✓	
David		✓
Sarah	✓	
Victor	✓	
Nicole		✓

2

■ Play the tape again. This time students write down the excuse that each person gives.

■ Students compare answers first with a partner, and then with the rest of the class.

Answers

David: He has to go out to dinner with his parents.
Nicole: She's going to (go to) a concert with her friend Robert.

10 READING 🔘

SB p. 105 This activity practices reading for specific information about weekend events.

1

■ Books open. Explain the task. Then students read the text silently to do the activity.

■ If students have problems with vocabulary, encourage them to guess the meaning from context. Alternatively, discuss the words as a class. Elicit the meanings from students, or mime/demonstrate the words.

■ If you wish, play the tape and have students listen and read to check their answers.

■ Students compare answers first with a partner, then with the class.

Answers

a) *buy clothes or jewelry:* Crafts Fair, Summer Fashion Show
b) *buy food:* Crafts Fair, Canine Club Show, Library Lecture Series
c) *sit indoors:* City Museum Travel Series, Library Lecture Series
d) *be outdoors:* Rock Concert, Crafts Fair

Note: The Canine Club Show and Summer Fashion Show could be either outdoors or indoors; the text does not say. However, the photo for the Canine Club Show indicates that it will take place outdoors.

2   Pair work

■ Explain the task. Students write down three activities from the reading they want to do.

■ Students compare their choices with a partner and find one activity they can do together. Encourage them to use the expression "want to."

■ Pairs report their choice to the class.

Extra practice

■ Bring in a weekend activities listing from a local English newspaper or magazine.

■ Students choose three things they want to do. Then they mix and mingle to invite classmates to join them. Encourage them to use the expression "Do you want to . . ." in their invitations.

■ When students find someone who wants to do the same thing, they join together.

■ As a class, figure out which activity is the most popular by looking to see which group is the biggest. (10 minutes)

Review of Units 13–16

This unit reviews the form verb + *to* + verb, the functions of asking for and giving directions, prepositions of place, and past tense verbs.

UNIT PLAN

1 Classroom Rules: *Reviews* have to *and contrasts it with* can't

2 Locations: *Reviews prepositions of place in reading maps and giving directions*

3 No, She Wasn't!: *Reviews past tense statements with* was *and* were

4 Tell Us About It: *Reviews verbs in the past tense in a fluency activity*

5 Listening: *Reviews various grammar points from these four units*

6 Future Plans: *Reviews the form verb* + to + *verb*

---

1 CLASSROOM RULES

SB p. 106 This activity reviews *have to* (obligation) and contrasts it with *can't* (prohibition).

■ Books open. Explain the task and go over the examples. Students work alone to write four classroom rules with *have to* and four with *can't*.

■ Students compare their rules with a partner.

■ Bring the class back together and ask students to read one of their rules to the class.

Sample answers

You have to sit down in a chair.
You have to do your homework.
You have to listen to the teacher.
You have to work with a partner.
You can't smoke.
You can't shout.
You can't fight.
You can't eat.

2 LOCATIONS

SB p. 106 This activity reviews prepositions of place and directions by having students talk about places on a map.

1 Pair work

■ Books open. Explain the task and model the sample language.

■ Pairs take turns giving the location of the places listed in different ways.

■ Pick a few places on the map. See how many different ways the class can give the location.

Sample answers

a) *parking lot:* The parking lot is on Second Avenue. It's between Third Avenue and Second Avenue. It's across from Park's Korean Barbecue.
b) *drugstore:* The drugstore is on Lincoln Street. It's between the Seattle Coffee Bar and Computer Wizards.

c) *night club:* The night club is on Second Avenue. It's between Lincoln Street and Jefferson Street. It's next to the Long Life Health Club. It's across from the movie theater.

d) *bus stop:* The bus stop is on the corner of Lincoln Street and Third Avenue. It's in front of the Seattle Coffee Bar.

e) *public restroom:* The public restroom is in front of the Discount Drugstore. It's on Lincoln Street.

2 Pair work

- Read the instructions to the class and model the sample conversation.

- Pairs take turns giving directions to a place on the map and saying where the directions lead.

3] NO, SHE WASN'T!

SB p. 106 This activity reviews past tense statements with *was* and *wasn't*.

1 Class activity

- Books open. Explain the task and go over the example.

- Students work alone to write three false statements about famous people from the past.

- Circulate to help with vocabulary and check for accuracy.

- Students take turns reading their false statements to the class. Ask for a volunteer to correct the statement, using the sample dialogue as a model. (In large classes, this can be done in groups.)

4] TELL US ABOUT IT

SB p. 107 This activity reviews past tense verbs in questions and answers about past activities.

Group work

- Books open. Explain the task. Give students a minute or two to make notes on the things they did last week.

- Form groups of four students. One student begins by making a statement about a weekend activity. The other three members of the group each must think of a question to ask about the activity. To demonstrate this, go over the sample conversation with the class.

- Bring the class back together, and have each student report on the activities of another group member.

5] LISTENING

SB p. 107 This activity reviews several grammar points from Units 13–16 by having students choose the best response to a question.

- Books open. Explain the task: Students listen to a question and choose the correct response. Read the responses.

- Play the tape as students do the task.

- Ask students to compare answers with a partner or in small groups. Then play the tape again so that students can check their work.

- Go over the answers with the class.

(instructions continue on next page)

Tape transcript

Listen and choose the correct response.

a) Were Brian and Victor in class last night?

b) What time did you go to work this morning?

c) Who did you go to the beach with on Saturday?

d) How was the party at Jennifer's?

e) We had a great barbecue on Sunday afternoon. Why didn't you go?

f) There's an interesting movie at the Odeon tonight. Do you want to go?

g) This is Stephanie calling. Is David there, please?

h) Is there a public restroom near here?

Answers

a) No, they weren't.
b) At eleven o'clock.
c) Amy and Katherine.
d) It was great.
e) Because I had a terrible headache.
f) I'm sorry, but I can't. I have to work.
g) I'm sorry, he's not here right now.
h) No, there isn't. Sorry.

Optional activity

■ Working in pairs, students write questions to go with the eight responses that were not correct in exercise 5.

■ Circulate to help with vocabulary and check for accuracy. Then pairs practice the questions and answers.

6 FUTURE PLANS

SB p. 107 This activity reviews the verb + *to* + verb form by having students write five sentences about things they want to do in the future.

■ Books open. Explain the task and go over the examples.

■ Students write five statements about things they want to do in the next five years.

■ Circulate to help with vocabulary and check for accuracy.

■ Students take turns reading their sentences to a partner.

■ Bring the class back together and have each student read aloud one of the things he or she wants to do.

Extra practice

■ Students write three sentences about things they don't want to do in the future. Then they compare sentences with a partner.

Tests

The following set of four tests may be used to assess students' mastery of the material presented in *Interchange Intro*. Each test covers four units. Not only will these tests allow you to determine how successfully the students have mastered the material, but the tests will also give the students a sense of accomplishment. For general information about these tests and about testing, see "Testing Students' Progress" on pages 8 and 9.

When to give a test

■ Give the appropriate test after students complete each cycle of four units and the accompanying review unit in the Student's Book.

Before giving a test

■ Photocopy the test for the students to take in class.

■ Schedule a class period of about 45 minutes to one hour for each test.

■ Locate the taped passage for the test listening section(s) on the Class Cassettes. The tests are at the end of the cassette set (side 6).

■ Tell the students they are going to have a "pencil and paper" test (i.e., oral production will not be tested) and suggest that they prepare for the test by reviewing the appropriate units. In studying for the test, students should pay particular attention to the grammar, conversations, and Word Power/vocabulary exercises. Remind students that the test will also contain short listening sections.

How to give a test

■ Explain that the point of the test is not to have students competing with each other for the highest grade; rather, the test will inform each student (and the teacher) how well the material was learned and what material may need extra review and practice.

■ Hand out one photocopy of the test to each student.

■ Allow about five minutes for the students to look through the test first, without answering any of the test items. Make sure students understand how to complete each section (e.g., fill in the blank, circle true or false, check the correct answer). Remind student to leave time at the end of the test for the listening section.

■ Remind students not to use their Student's Books or dictionaries during the test.

■ To help students use their time efficiently and to finish on time, write the total time for the test on the board before beginning the test: 45 minutes.

■ After the test begins, revise the time remaining every ten minutes to show students how much time is left.

■ Play the tape for the listening section(s) twice. Students listen only the first time, and then listen and mark their answers during the second playing.

■ If you do not wish to use class time for the test, tell students to complete everything at home except the listening item(s). Remind them to complete the test at home in 40 minutes and not to use the Student's Book or dictionary. In class, play the taped section(s) and then score the test.

How to score a test

■ Either collect the tests and use the Answer Key to score them, or go over the test with the class.

■ Each test is worth a total of 100 points. If you wish to give a grade, use this scoring system:

```
90–100 points = A or Excellent
 80–89 points = B or Very Good
 70–79 points = C or Fair
  69 or below = Need to review units
```

Name _____

Date _____

1. Write *am*, *'m*, *are*, *'re*, *is*, or *'s*.

a) That's David's friend. His name _____ John.

b) What _____ these called in English?

c) Your wallet _____ on the table.

d) _____ these your keys?

e) I _____ not from the United States.

f) _____ I right?

g) _____ she your teacher?

h) The notebooks _____ next to the pencils.

i) They _____ from Japan.

j) _____ it cloudy today?

2. Circle the correct word.

a) What's your name?

  (**My** / **I**) name is Michael.

b) What color is your classroom?

  (**Our** / **Their**) classroom is blue.

c) What's her brother's name?

  (**Her** / **His**) name is Steven.

d) What's your friend's name?

  (**She** / **Her**) name is Katherine.

e) What's David and Michael's telephone number?

  (**Their** / **They**) telephone number is 555-8975.

f) Where is your book?

  (**Your** / **My**) book is in my bag.

3. Listen to the conversations. Are the phone numbers correct or incorrect? Check (✓) the answer. If incorrect, write the correct number. ▭

		Correct	*Incorrect*	*Correct number*
a)	555-9144	☐	☐	_____
b)	555-8927	☐	☐	_____
c)	555-3146	☐	☐	_____
d)	555-6182	☐	☐	_____

4. Write the correct number for each word.

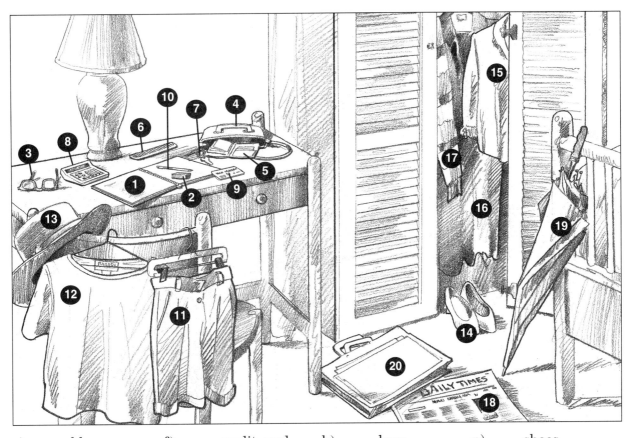

a) ____ blouse
b) ____ briefcase
c) ____ calculator
d) ____ coat
e) ____ comb

f) ____ credit card
g) ____ eraser
h) ____ glasses
i) ____ handbag
j) ____ hat

k) ____ keys
l) ____ newspaper
m) ____ notebook
n) ____ pencil
o) ____ scarf

p) ____ shoes
q) ____ shorts
r) ____ T-shirt
s) ____ umbrella
t) ____ wallet

5. Complete the sentences with *in*, *of*, *from*, *to*, or *on*.

a) Korea is _____ Asia.

b) Marta isn't Brazilian. She's _____ Mexico.

c) Her newspaper is _____ Spanish.

d) The book is in front _____ the television.

e) The chair is next _____ the sofa.

f) Write your name _____ the board.

g) My credit cards are _____ my wallet.

h) Are you _____ my math class?

i) Jennifer's comb is _____ the table.

j) What is the weather like _____ your city?

6. Read the sentences about the pictures. Circle *T* for True or *F* for False.

a) **T F** The newspaper is under the table.

d) **T F** The glasses are on the handbag.

b) **T F** The keys are on the television.

e) **T F** The umbrella is behind the chair.

c) **T F** The comb is in front of the wallet.

f) **T F** The notebook is next to the keys.

7. Write the verb in present continuous.

a) We _____ _____(wear) tennis shoes today.

b) The teacher _____ _____(carry) a brown briefcase.

c) Sarah _____ _____(read) a newspaper.

d) It's cold, so I _____ _____(take) a taxi.

e) They _____ _____(run) in the park.

8. Write the questions.

a) _____?
No, I'm not Michael. I'm Brian.

b) _____?
Yes, they're my keys. Thanks.

c) _____?
They're called "tissues" in English.

d) _____?
No, they're not Jennifer's sunglasses. They're Lisa's.

e) _____?
Your keys are on the table.

f) _____?
No, Brazil is in South America, not Central America.

g) _____?
No, Bob's not from the United States. He's from Canada.

h) _____?
My running shoes are gray.

9. Listen to the conversations and check (✓) the answers.

a) Susan's last name is ☐ Moss. She is a ☐ student.
☐ Morse. ☐ teacher.

b) This calculator belongs to ☐ David. David's calculator is ☐ gray.
☐ Steven. ☐ black.

c) Today it's ☐ sunny. Jennifer and her friends are ☐ swimming.
☐ raining. ☐ running.

d) William's telephone number is ☐ 555-9163. He lives with ☐ his parents.
☐ 555-5173. ☐ his friend.

e) It's ☐ 30 degrees Fahrenheit. The season is ☐ fall.
☐ 13 degrees Fahrenheit. ☐ winter.

Name _____

Date _____

1. Write the times. Don't use numerals.

Example: It's twenty-five to eleven.

a) _____

d) _____

b) _____

e) _____

c) _____

f) _____

2. Circle the correct word.

a) My parents (**live / lives**) downtown.

b) My mother (**wear / wears**) glasses.

c) My father (**go / goes**) to work by car.

d) I don't (**live / lives**) downtown.

e) My sister (**doesn't / don't**) use public transportation.

f) I (**watch / watches**) television on Sunday.

g) My parents (**doesn't / don't**) watch television.

h) We (**get up / gets up**) at 7:30.

3. Write short answers to the questions.

a) Are you working today? No, _____ .

b) Is Sue sleeping? Yes, _____ .

c) Are they having dinner with us tonight? Yes, _____ .

d) Does Jennifer live with her parents? No, _____ .

e) Do Brian and David live near here? Yes, _____ .

f) Do you have a car? No, _____ .

4. Complete the questions with *do*, *does*, *am*, *are*, or *is*.

a) What time _____ it in Chicago now?

b) What _____ Bob and Sue reading?

c) What color tie _____ I wearing?

d) Where _____ she work?

e) Who _____ making breakfast today?

f) What _____ your parents do?

g) How _____ she going to school?

h) What _____ they doing?

i) Where _____ he live? In the city or in the suburbs?

j) What _____ you eat for breakfast?

5. Write the questions.

a) A: Where _____ ?
    B: My parents work downtown.

b) A: What _____ ?
    B: I'm reading an interesting book.

c) A: Where _____ ?
    B: My sister lives in Texas.

d) A: Is _____ ?
    B: Yes, there's a desk in the bedroom.

e) A: Are _____ ?
    B: No, I'm not having breakfast. I'm having lunch.

f) A: Where _____ ?
    B: He's going to Taiwan.

145

6. Write the days of the week, in order.

a) _____   e) _____

b) _____   f) _____

c) _____   g) _____

d) _____

7. Write the correct number for each word.

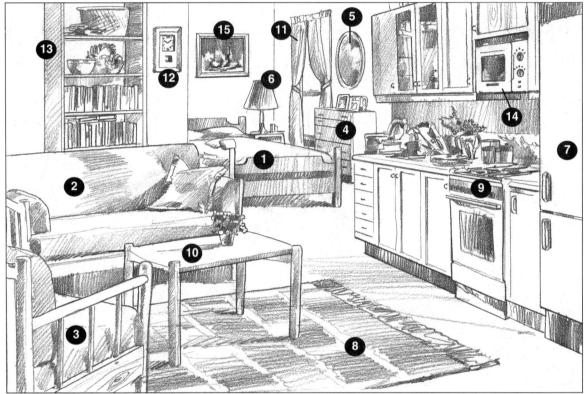

a) ____ armchair   e) ____ curtains   i) ____ mirror   m) ____ sofa

b) ____ bed   f) ____ dresser   j) ____ picture   n) ____ stove

c) ____ bookcase   g) ____ lamp   k) ____ refrigerator   o) ____ table

d) ____ clock   h) ____ microwave oven   l) ____ rug

8. Complete the sentences with *at*, *in*, or *on*.

a) I have breakfast ____ 7:45.

b) I don't work ____ Saturday.

c) I take the bus ____ the morning.

d) I don't get up early ____ the weekend.

e) I get home ____ nine o'clock every night.

f) I watch television ____ the evening.

9. What are their jobs?

Example: <u>He's a doctor.</u>

a) _____   b) _____   c) _____

d) _____   e) _____   f) _____

10. Answer the questions with opposites.

Example: Is her job pleasant? <u>No, it's unpleasant.</u>

a) Is a police officer's job safe?   No, _____ .

b) Is your job interesting?   No, _____ .

c) Is a pilot's job relaxing?   No, _____ .

d) Is a teacher's job easy?   No, _____ .

e) Is a lawyer's salary low?   No, _____ .

11. Listen to the conversations and check (✓) the correct answers. 🔘

a) Jim goes to work   ☐ at 6:00 A.M.   He's   ☐ a pilot.
                   ☐ at 6:30 A.M.   ☐ a police officer.

    His job is   ☐ boring.   He lives   ☐ in the city.
              ☐ stressful.   ☐ in the suburbs.

b) Katherine's apartment   ☐ doesn't have a view.   It's next to   ☐ the river.
                          ☐ has a view.   ☐ the park.

    It has   ☐ one bedroom.   Katherine needs   ☐ a sofa.
          ☐ two bedrooms.   ☐ some curtains.

1. Complete the sentences with *is* or *are*.

a)   Rice _____ popular in my country.

b)   Strawberries _____ his favorite food.

c)   Cheese _____ good for you.

d)   Potatoes _____ my favorite starch.

e)   I think yogurt _____ delicious.

f)   My favorite vegetables _____ green beans and broccoli.

2. Circle the wrong word in each list.

a) *Vegetables*	b) *Fruit*	c) *Meat*	d) *Dairy foods*
carrots	mangoes	beef	bread
peppers	apples	pasta	milk
oranges	bananas	lamb	butter
beans	broccoli	chicken	yogurt

3. Circle the correct words.

a)   We're cooking (**some** / **any**) vegetables.

b)   There's no butter. We need (**some** / **any**).

c)   We don't need (**some** / **any**) bread, but we need some rice.

d)   Do you want (**some** / **any**) milk in your coffee?

4. Put the words in the right order.

a)   breakfast / I / coffee / often / for / have .

_____

b)   ever / fish / breakfast / you / do / eat / for ?

_____

c)   we / Sunday / on / have / big / a / breakfast / always .

_____

d)   dinner / usually / you / what / have / time / do ?

_____

5. Complete the sentences with the words *too*, *either*, *but*, or *and*.

a) Bob can cook. Sam can cook, _____ .

b) I can cook fish, _____ I can't cook meat very well.

c) I can't swim. I can't dive, _____ .

d) I can play the piano. I can play the guitar, _____ .

e) Rosa can speak Spanish _____ French.

f) I can play Ping-Pong, _____ I can't play tennis.

6. Sam is the same as you. Write sentences about Sam.

    Example: I can dance. *Sam can dance.*

a) I'm not good at writing poetry.

    Sam _____ .

b) I know how to play basketball.

    _____ .

c) I can play the piano very well.

    _____ .

d) I don't know how to play chess.

    _____ .

e) I can't speak Arabic, but I'm good at French.

    _____ .

f) I'm good at card games. I can play ten different games!

    _____ .

7. Write the dates.

Example: 9/11 *September eleventh*

a) 6/15 _____

b) 2/22 _____

c) 12/25 _____

d) 7/28 _____

e) 4/6 _____

f) 1/16 _____

8. Write the questions.

a) _____?

I'm going to watch television tonight.

b) _____?

No, I can't swim.

c) _____?

Yes, I'm good at cooking.

d) _____?

I'm going to study Spanish next year.

e) _____?

Yes, I'm going to go out for my birthday.

f) _____?

No, she doesn't know how to play chess.

9. Check (✓) the best response.

a) I have a headache.

☐ That's a good idea.
☐ Oh, that's too bad.

b) I feel great today.

☐ What's wrong?
☐ That's good.

c) I have a terrible cold.

☐ Stay in bed and rest.
☐ Go swimming.

d) I feel better today.

☐ I'm glad to hear that.
☐ Take some aspirin.

e) Are you feeling better?

☐ Yes, thank you.
☐ No, I don't.

f) I can't sleep at night.

☐ That's fine.
☐ Don't drink coffee.

Test 3, page 4

10. Give advice. Use the words in parentheses ( ).

Example: I have a headache. (aspirin) *Take some aspirin.*

a) I want to lose weight. (desserts) _____ .

b) I have the flu. (bed) _____ .

c) My job is very stressful. (hot bath) _____ .

d) I have a sore throat. (talk) _____ .

e) I can't sleep. (coffee) _____ .

f) I'm hungry. (restaurant) _____ .

11. Complete the sentences with *in*, *on*, or *at*.

a) The party is _____ Wednesday night _____ 8:00 P.M.

b) I work _____ the weekends _____ December.

c) Let's meet _____ noon _____ Wednesday.

d) I go to bed late _____ night _____ the summer.

e) Please come to the office _____ Tuesday _____ two o'clock.

12. Listen to the conversations and check (✓) the information.

a) Barbara can ☐ swim.   Tom can ☐ dive and swim.
☐ dive.   ☐ drive.

b) On Saturday, Bob is going to ☐ rent a movie.   Jane is going to ☐ play tennis.
☐ play tennis.   ☐ study.

c) Lisa ☐ sometimes has a big lunch.   She usually eats ☐ salad.
☐ never   ☐ soup.

d) David has a ☐ headache.   He's going to ☐ take some aspirin.
☐ stomachache.   ☐ go to bed.

e) Mary is busy on ☐ Thursday.   The women are going to the movies on ☐ Friday night.
☐ Saturday.   ☐ the weekend.

152

Copyright © Cambridge University Press

1. Look at the map and complete the sentences.

a) The bank is _____ the post office.

b) The bookstore is _____ the coffee shop.

c) The subway is _____ Stanford Street and Second Avenue.

d) The hotel is _____ Yale Street and Cornell Street.

e) The gas station is _____ the supermarket.

f) The parking lot is _____ the hotel.

Test 4, page 2

2. Look at the map in part 1. Circle the incorrect word or expression in these directions. Write the correct word.

a) You are at the coffee shop. You want to go to the subway. Walk up Third Avenue for two blocks. Turn right. Walk one block. The subway is on your right.

correct word or expression: _____

b) You are at the subway station. You want to go to the bank. Walk up Second Avenue for two blocks. Turn left. It's on the right, across from the post office.

correct word or expression: _____

c) You are at the hotel. To get to the post office, walk up Third Avenue to Yale Street and turn left. Walk one and a half blocks. It's on the left.

correct word or expression: _____

3. Complete the sentences with the past or present tense.

  Example: I *ate* lunch, but I didn't eat breakfast.

a) Bill _____ broccoli, but he doesn't like green beans.

b) Jennifer saw Mary, but she _____ Lisa.

c) Katherine _____ to France last year. She also went to Greece.

d) David and Michael are going shopping because they _____ any food.

e) Kumiko_____ last night, but Nicole didn't study.

f) Did you watch television yesterday? No, I _____ television.

g) I _____ to my parents last week, but I didn't write to my grandparents.

h) Bob often _____ pizza, but Mark doesn't eat pizza very often.

4. Write the questions.

a) _____?
Yes, I worked on Saturday.

b) _____?
No, I don't need to see a doctor.

c) _____?
Yes, I had a good weekend, thanks.

d) _____?
Yes, I want to go to the gym.

e) _____?
No, I went to bed early last night.

f) _____?
Yes, I can play basketball very well.

5. Write the years.

Example: 1767 *seventeen sixty-seven*

a) 1993 _____   d) 1903 _____

b) 1951 _____   e) 1899 _____

c) 1940 _____   f) 1530 _____

6. Complete the sentences with *was* or *were*.

a) _____ you born in this city?

b) Where _____ your parents born?

c) My father _____ born in this country.

d) What _____ your favorite subject in high school?

e) When _____ your sister married?

f) Who _____ your best friends in high school?

Test 4, page 4

7. Write the questions.

a) _____?

My favorite teacher in high school was Mrs. Brown.

b) _____?

I went to college in California.

c) _____?

My father is fifty years old.

d) _____?

I went shopping because I needed food.

e) _____?

My vacation was great!

f) _____?

History was my favorite subject in high school.

8. Complete the sentences with *at*, *in*, or *on*.

a) Are you _____ vacation this week?

b) Is Lisa _____ work today?

c) Bob is sick. He's _____ bed.

d) I bought these shoes _____ the mall.

e) Susan is _____ Europe this month.

f) John likes to sing _____ the shower.

9. Complete the sentences with object pronouns.

Example: Tom and I like to play tennis. I play with *him* every week.

a) I called Mary and left _____ a message.

b) This is John's umbrella. Please give it to _____ .

c) This is a great book. Do you want to read _____ ?

d) Do you know the Smiths? I invited _____ to dinner.

e) We're going to the beach. Do you want to come with _____ ?

f) He came to see _____ yesterday, but I wasn't home.

10. Circle the correct words.

a) My mother doesn't (**likes** / **like**) to go to the movies.

b) I want (**to see** / **see**) a movie tonight.

c) I'm on vacation. I don't (**have** / **have to**) go to work.

d) We (**needs** / **need**) to save some money.

e) Can you (**go** / **to go**) to a restaurant tonight?

f) She doesn't (**know how to** / **know to**) swim.

11. Listen to the conversations and check (✓) the correct answers. 🖭

a) Maria was born in ☐ the United States.   She moved to Chicago when she was ☐ 16.
☐ Chile.   ☐ 15.

b) Bill wants to ☐ go to a club.   But he has to ☐ study for a test.
☐ go to sleep early.   ☐ go out with some friends.

c) Christine is looking for ☐ a restaurant.   She's on ☐ Prince Street and Second Avenue.
☐ a movie theater.   ☐ Prince Street and Third Avenue.

Tape Transcripts for Tests

Test 1: Units 1–4

3 Listen to the conversations. Are the numbers correct or incorrect? If incorrect, write the correct number.

a)
A: What's your telephone number?
B: It's 555-5144.
A: Thanks.

b)
A: Your phone number, please?
B: My number is 555-8927.

c)
A: What's your phone number?
B: It's 555-3146.
A: Thanks.

d)
A: My number is 555-6183.
B: Thank you very much.

9 Listen to the conversations and check the answers.

a)
A: Hello. My name's John Price.
B: I'm Susan Morse.
A: Susan Moss?
B: No, Morse. M–O–R–S–E.
A: Nice to meet you, Susan. Are you a student?
B: No, actually, I'm your teacher!
A: Oh, you're *Ms.* Morse, then. I'm sorry.
B: That's OK.

b)
A: Hi, David. Is this your calculator?
B: No, my calculator is black. I think this is Steven's calculator.
A: Where's Steven?
B: He's over there. He's wearing a gray shirt.

c)
[*sound of footsteps on gravel and labored breathing*]
MAN: Come on, Jennifer! Running is great exercise!
WOMAN: All right, all right. I'm coming. Oh, I'm tired.
    [*sound of thunder and rain*]
MAN: Oh, no! It's raining.
WOMAN: Good. Let's stop!

d)
A: What's your telephone number, William?
B: It's 555-5173.
A: OK, great. By the way, do you live with your parents?
B: No, I live with a friend, John. His brother Brian is in your class.

e)
A: Are you all right, Linda?
B: Yes, I'm OK. But it's so cold!
A: It *is* cold. It's thirty degrees Fahrenheit.
B: Thirty degrees! It's very cold this fall.

Test 2: Units 5–8

11 Listen to the conversations and check the correct answers.

a)
WOMAN: Do you get up early, Jim?
JIM: Yeah, I get up around six A.M. I go to work at six thirty.
WOMAN: Really? Do you work in the city?
JIM: No. I'm a pilot.
WOMAN: Wow! That's an interesting job.
JIM: Yes, it is, but it's very stressful.
WOMAN: Do you live near the airport?
JIM: No, I live in the suburbs. It's more relaxing there!

b)
[*the friend is female*]
FRIEND: How's your new apartment, Katherine?
KATHERINE: It's lovely, thanks. There's a great view of the park from my window.
FRIEND: Oh, you're so lucky. My apartment doesn't have a view.
KATHERINE: So come and live with me. I'm looking for a roommate. And I have two bedrooms.
FRIEND: Really?
KATHERINE: Yes, but I don't have anything to sit on! I need a sofa and some chairs.

Test 3: Units 9–12

12 Listen to the conversations and check the information.

a)
TOM: Hi, Barbara.
BARBARA: Oh, hi, Tom.
TOM: Do you want to go to the pool?
BARBARA: I'm . . . um . . . I'm not sure.
TOM: Why not? It's so hot today.
BARBARA: Well, I can swim, but not very well. And I can't dive.
TOM: No problem. I know how to swim and dive. I can help you.
BARBARA: OK, great!

b)
JANE: What are you going to do on Saturday, Bob?
BOB: I'm going to rent a movie. What about you?
JANE: Well, I usually play tennis on Saturday, but this weekend I'm going to study. I have a test on Monday.
BOB: Oh, that's too bad. But good luck with your test!

c)
MAN: Hey, let's go out for lunch, Lisa.
LISA: Oh, no thanks. I have a salad with me.
MAN: Just a salad?
LISA: Yeah, I never eat a big lunch. I love vegetables, so I usually have a salad.
MAN: Well, I think I'm going to buy some soup and a sandwich. See you later!

d)
WOMAN: What's the matter, David?
DAVID: Oh, I have a terrible headache.
WOMAN: That's too bad. Why don't you take some aspirin?
DAVID: No, I don't usually take aspirin. I think I'm just going to go to bed.
WOMAN: Well, OK. I hope you feel better soon!

e)
WOMAN: Can you go out on Thursday or Friday, Mary?
MARY: No, sorry. I'm busy both nights.
WOMAN: Well, how about doing something on the weekend?
MARY: Let's see. I'm busy all day on Sunday, but I'm not doing anything on Saturday.
WOMAN: Why don't we go to a restaurant on Saturday night?
MARY: Actually, I'm on a diet. Let's go see a movie instead.

Test 4: Units 13–16

11 Listen to the conversations and check the correct answers.

a)
MAN: Were you born in Chicago, Maria?
MARIA: No, I wasn't. I was born in Santiago, in Chile.
MAN: Really? When did you come to Chicago?
MARIA: When I was sixteen. My parents moved to the United States.
MAN: Well, I'm glad you came!
MARIA: Me too.

b)
[*phone rings*]
BILL: [*answering phone*] Hello.
JOHN: Oh, hi, Bill. It's John. Do you want to go out tonight?
BILL: Hm. Where are you going?
JOHN: I'm going to a club with some friends.
BILL: Oh, gee, it sounds really great. I want to come, but I have to study.
JOHN: Are you sure?
BILL: Well, maybe . . . No, I'm sorry. You see, there's a test tomorrow and I really have to study for it.

c)
JIM: Hi, Christine. How are things going?
CHRISTINE: Oh, hi, Jim. Well, actually, not great. I'm lost.
JIM: Maybe I can help you. Where are you going?
CHRISTINE: I'm going to the Regency Theater. But I don't have the address.
JIM: The Regency. Oh, that's easy. See, we're on Prince Street and Second Avenue now, and the Regency is on Prince and Third. Just walk one block on Prince.
CHRISTINE: Oh, thanks, Jim. I'm glad I saw you!
JIM: Bye. Enjoy the movie!

Answer Keys for Tests

Test 1

1.
a) is   e) 'm (am)   h) are
b) are   f) Am   i) 're (are)
c) is   g) Is   j) Is
d) Are

[10 x 1 = 10]

2.
a) My b) Our c) His d) Her e) Their f) My

[6 x 1 = 6]

3.
a) incorrect; 555-5144
b) correct
c) correct
d) incorrect; 555-6183

[4 x 1 = 4]

4.
a) 15   h) 3   o) 17
b) 20   i) 4   p) 14
c) 8   j) 13   q) 11
d) 16   k) 7   r) 12
e) 6   l) 18   s) 19
f) 9   m) 1   t) 5
g) 2   n) 10

[20 x 1 = 20]

5.
a) in   d) of   g) in   i) on
b) from e) to   h) in   j) in
c) in   f) on

[10 x 1 = 10]

6.
a) F   b) T   c) F   d) T   e) F   f) T

[6 x 1 = 6]

7.
a) are wearing *or* 're wearing
b) is carrying *or* 's carrying
c) is reading *or* 's reading
d) am taking *or* 'm taking
e) are running *or* 're running

[5 x 2 = 10]

8.
a) Are you Michael?
b) Are these your keys?
c) What are these called in English?
d) Are these Jennifer's sunglasses?
e) Where are my keys?
f) Is Brazil in Central America?
g) Is Bob from the United States?
h) What color are your running shoes?

[8 x 3 = 24]

9.
a) Morse, teacher
b) Steven, black
c) raining, running
d) 555-5173, his friend
e) 30 degrees Fahrenheit, fall

[5 x 2 = 10]

Test 2

1.
Note: Only the expressions given in the Student's Book are listed as answers. If you discussed variants with your class, you can accept them as answers as well.

a) It's a quarter to three. *or* It's two forty-five.
b) It's twelve thirty.
c) It's ten minutes after seven.
d) It's twenty-five after nine. *or* It's nine twenty-five.
e) It's a quarter after three. *or* It's three-fifteen.
f) It's twenty-five to nine. *or* It's eight thirty-five.

[6 x 1 = 6]

2.
a) live   c) goes   e) doesn't   g) don't
b) wears d) live   f) watch   h) get up

[8 x 1 = 8]

3.
a) No, I'm not.   d) No, she doesn't.
b) Yes, she is.   e) Yes, they do.
c) Yes, they are.   f) No, I don't.

[6 x 2 = 12]

4.
a) is   d) does   g) is   i) does
b) are   e) is   h) are   j) do
c) am   f) do

[10 x 1 = 10]

5.
a) Where do your parents work?
b) What are you reading? / What are you doing?
c) Where does your sister live?
d) Is there a desk in the bedroom?
e) Are you having breakfast?
f) Where is he going?

[6 x 2 = 12]

6.
a) Sunday
b) Monday
c) Tuesday
d) Wednesday
e) Thursday
f) Friday
g) Saturday

[6 x 1 = 6]

7.
a) 3   d) 12   g) 6   j) 15   m) 2
b) 1   e) 11   h) 14   k) 7   n) 9
c) 13   f) 4   i) 5   l) 8   o) 10

[15 x 1 = 15]

8.
a) at   c) in   e) at
b) on   d) on   f) in

[6 x 1 = 6]

9.
a) He's a waiter.
b) They're musicians.
c) They're chefs / cooks.
d) She's a nurse.
e) He's a security guard.
f) She's a police officer.

[6 x 2 = 12]

10.
a) No, it's dangerous.
b) No, it's boring (*or* uninteresting).
c) No, it's stressful.
d) No, it's difficult.
e) No, it's high.

[5 x 1 = 5]

11.
a) at 6:30 A.M. / a pilot / stressful / in the suburbs
b) has a view / the park / two bedrooms / a sofa

[8 x 1 = 8]

Test 3

1.
a) is   b) are   c) is   d) are   e) is   f) are

[6 x 1 = 6]

2.
a) oranges   b) broccoli   c) pasta   d) bread

[4 x 1 = 4]

3.
a) some   b) some   c) any   d) any

[4 x 1 = 4]

4.
a) I often have coffee for breakfast.
b) Do you ever eat fish for breakfast?
c) We always have a big breakfast on Sunday.
d) What time do you usually have dinner?

[4 x 3 = 12]

5.
a) too   c) either   e) and
b) but   d) too   f) but

[6 x 1 = 6]

6.
a) Sam isn't good at writing poetry.
b) Sam knows how to play basketball.
c) Sam can play the piano very well.
d) Sam doesn't know how to play chess.
e) Sam can't speak Arabic, but he's good at French.
f) Sam is good at card games. He can play ten different games!

[6 x 1 = 6]

7.
a) June fifteenth
b) February twenty-second
c) December twenty-fifth
d) July twenty-eighth
e) April sixth
f) January sixteenth

[6 x 2 = 12]

8.
a) What are you going to do tonight?
b) Can you swim?
c) Are you good at cooking?
d) What are you going to study next year?
e) Are you going to go out for your birthday?
f) Does she know how to play chess?

[6 x 3 = 18]

9.
a) Oh, that's too bad.
b) That's good.
c) Stay in bed and rest.
d) I'm glad to hear that.
e) Yes, thank you.
f) Don't drink coffee.

[6 x 1 = 6]

10.
a) Don't eat desserts.
b) Stay in bed. / Go to bed.
c) Take a hot bath.
d) Don't talk.
e) Don't drink coffee (at night).
f) Go (out) to a restaurant.

[6 x 1 = 6]

11.
a) on, at   c) at, on   e) on, at
b) on, in   d) at, in

[5 x 2 = 10]

12.
a) swim, dive and swim
b) rent a movie, study
c) never, salad
d) headache, go to bed
e) Thursday, the weekend

[5 x 2 = 10]

Test 4

1.
a) next to   d) between
b) across from   e) in front of
c) on the corner of f) behind

[6 x 1 = 6]

2.
a) Walk *up*. should be Walk *down*.
b) *across from* should be *next to*
c) *on the left* should be *on the right*

[3 x 2 = 6]

3.
a) likes   e) studied
b) didn't see   f) didn't watch
c) went   g) wrote
d) don't have h) eats

[8 x 2 = 16]

4.
a) Did you work on Saturday?
b) Do you need to see a doctor?
c) Did you have a good weekend?
d) Do you want to go to the gym?
e) Did you go to bed late last night?
f) Can you play basketball?

[6 x 2 = 12]

5.
a) nineteen ninety-three
b) nineteen fifty-one
c) nineteen forty
d) nineteen-oh-three (*or* nineteen hundred and three)
e) eighteen ninety-nine
f) fifteen thirty

[6 x 1 = 6]

6.
a) Were   c) was   e) was
b) were   d) was   f) were

[6 x 1 = 6]

7.
a) Who was your favorite teacher in high school?
b) Where did you go to college?
c) How old is your father?
d) Why did you go shopping?
e) How was your vacation?
f) What was your favorite subject in high school?

[6 x 3 = 18]

8.
a) on   b) at   c) in   d) at   e) in   f) in

[6 x 1 = 6]

9.
a) her   b) him   c) it   d) them   e) us   f) me

[6 x 1 = 6]

10.
a) like   c) have to   e) go
b) to see   d) need   f) know how to

[6 x 1 = 6]

11.
a) Chile, 16
b) go to a club, study for a test
c) a movie theater, Prince Street and Second Avenue

[6 x 2 = 12]

Workbook Answer Key

Unit 1
Hello. My name is Jennifer Wan.

1.
Answers will vary.

2.
b) Her name is Liz Gray.
c) His name is Bobby.
d) Her name is Sue Ray.
e) His name is Toshi.
f) His name is Frank Price.

3.
b) are
c) is
d) is
e) are
f) is
g) is
h) are

4.
b) It's your book.
c) You're in my math class.
d) He's over there.
e) What's your last name?
f) We're students.

5.
Sarah: Excuse me, are you Michael Lynch?
Robert: No, I'm not. He's over there.
Sarah: Oh, I'm sorry.

Sarah: Excuse me, Michael. I think this is your book.
Michael: That's right! It's my math book. Thank you!
     By the way, are you in my math class?
Sarah: Yes, I am. My name is Sarah Smith.

6.
b) two
c) one
d) four
e) zero
f) seven
g) five
h) six
i) nine
j) three
l) 3735
m) 1156
n) 5302

7.
b) This is a chair.
c) This is a table.
d) This is a desk.
e) This is a wastebasket.
f) This is a book.
g) This is an umbrella.
h) This is an eraser.

8.
b) M-O-O-R-E.
c) You're right. Thanks.
d) 555-4553.
e) Good-bye. Have a nice day.

9.
b) Find the word *briefcase*.
c) Take out your (*or* a) pen.
d) Go to the board. (*or* Please go to the board.)
e) Write the word *briefcase* on the board.

Unit 2
What's this called in English?

1.
b) This is Ryan's briefcase.
c) This is Amanda's umbrella.
d) These are Amanda's keys.
e) This is Ryan's notebook.
f) These are Ryan's pens.
g) These are Amanda's books.
h) This is Ryan's calculator.

2.

/s/	/z/	/ɪz/
maps	photos	briefcases
wallets	umbrellas	glasses
desks	pens	addresses
	tissues	licenses
	keys	

3.
a)
Lauren: Hi, Andrea! Is this your umbrella?
Andrea: No, my umbrella is different. Maybe it's
     Robert's.
Lauren: You're right. It *is* his umbrella. And these are
     his sunglasses, too.
Andrea: No, I think they're Lynn's. Her name is on the
     case.
Lauren: Hmm. Are Robert and Lynn here today?
Andrea: I don't know. But their lockers are over there.

b)
Pete: Hi, Anita. Hi, Ellen. Are you in <u>my</u> history class?
Ellen: I think we're in <u>your</u> class.
Pete: Great. Where is <u>our</u> classroom?
Ellen: It's over there. But <u>our</u> class is tomorrow, not today!

4.
b)
Hi. <u>Are</u> these your glasses?
<u>No, my glasses are different.</u>
c)
Excuse me. <u>Is</u> this Mrs. Miller's class?
<u>Yes, it is. And</u> I'm Mrs. Miller.
d)
Hello. <u>Is</u> this your dictionary?
<u>Yes, it is.</u> Thank you. <u>My name is right there.</u>
e)
<u>Is</u> this an English book?
<u>No, it's a French book.</u>
f)
<u>Are</u> these Andrea's keys?
<u>No, they're not her keys. They're Darryl's.</u>

5.
b) The keys are <u>on the table.</u>
c) The umbrella <u>is behind the chair.</u>
d) The wastebasket <u>is under the desk.</u>
e) The tissues <u>are in front of the wastebasket / are on the floor.</u>
f) The newspaper <u>is in the wastebasket.</u>
Answers will vary for (g)–(j). Sample answers:
The remote control is on the chair.
The handbag is next to the desk / table.
The hairbrush is in the handbag.
The photos are on the desk / next to the pens.
The pens are on the desk / next to the photos.
The wallet is on the television.

Unit 3
Where are you from?

1.
c) India <u>is in Asia.</u>
d) Costa Rica <u>is in Central America.</u>
e) Egypt <u>is in Africa.</u>
f) Greece <u>is in Europe.</u>
g) Malaysia and Indonesia <u>are in Asia.</u>
h) Chile <u>is in South America.</u>
i) The United States <u>is in North America.</u>
j) Korea <u>is in Asia.</u>

2.
b) Mexican
c) Turkish
d) Canadian
e) Indonesia
f) Ireland

3.
a)
A: Is your family from Korea?
B: No, they aren't from Korea. They<u>'re</u> from China.
A: <u>Are</u> your parents in China now?
B: <u>No</u>, they <u>aren't</u>. They<u>'re</u> in the United States.
b)
A: <u>Is</u> this your wallet?
B: <u>Yes</u>, it <u>is</u>. Thanks.
A: What about your credit cards? <u>Are</u> they there?
B: No, they <u>aren't</u>. They<u>'re</u> in my book bag.
c)
A: <u>Is</u> Peru in Central America?
B: <u>No</u>, it <u>isn't</u> in Central America. It<u>'s</u> in South America.
A: Oh, right. My geography <u>isn't</u> very good!
d)
A: What <u>are</u> these called in English? Are they called "mouthbrushes"?
B: No, they <u>aren't</u>. They<u>'re</u> called toothbrushes.
A: Thanks.

4.

Country	Nationality	Language
Vietnam	<u>Vietnamese</u>	Vietnamese
China	<u>Chinese</u>	<u>Chinese</u>
<u>Mexico</u>	Mexican	<u>Spanish</u>
<u>France</u>	French	<u>French</u>
Egypt	<u>Egyptian</u>	Arabic
Russia	<u>Russian</u>	Russian
Austria	<u>Austrian</u>	German
Japan	<u>Japanese</u>	Japanese
Brazil	Brazilian	<u>Portuguese</u>
Australia	Australian	<u>Australian</u>

5.

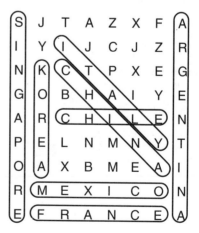

Answers will vary for (c)–(h), but sentences will follow these patterns:
(Name of language) is the language of (name of country).
(Name of country) is in (name of continent).
A person from (name of country) is (nationality).

6.
b) No, she isn't. / No, she's not.
c) No, they aren't. / No, they're not.
d) No, it isn't. / No, it's not.
e) Yes, it is.
f) Yes, I am. / No, I'm not. (Answers will vary.)

7.
b) Is your first name Lisa?
Yes, it is. / No, it isn't. (No, it's not.)
c) Are you and your family from Asia?
Yes, we are. / No, we aren't. (No, we're not.)
d) Are Michael and David English names?
Yes, they are.
e) Are your keys in your bag?
Yes, they are. / No, they aren't. (No, they're not.)
f) Is Whitney Houston American?
Yes, she is.

Unit 4
Clothes and weather

1.
Answers will vary.

2.
(*Note:* Accept any reasonable answer.)
c) Sarah and Victor are wearing hats.
d) David and Michael are wearing running shoes.
e) Victor and Nicole are wearing T-shirts.
f) Nicole is wearing slacks.
g) Jennifer, David, and Michael are wearing bathing suits.

3.
b) Victor is writing.
c) David is running.
d) Jennifer is swimming.
e) Sarah and Michael are playing ball.

4.
b) Elizabeth isn't wearing a coat. She's wearing a shirt.
c) Tom isn't playing tennis. He's running.
d) Bob and Cynthia aren't wearing winter clothes. They're wearing summer clothes.

5.
b) sixty
c) forty
d) seventy-eight
e) seven
f) twenty-one
g) thirty-two
h) thirteen

6.
The order of answers will vary.
b) It's raining in San Francisco. The temperature is forty-six degrees Fahrenheit (eight degrees Celsius).
c) It's sunny in Los Angeles. The temperature is fifty degrees Fahrenheit (ten degrees Celsius).
d) It's sunny in Houston. The temperature is fifty-nine degrees Fahrenheit (fifteen degrees Celsius).
e) It's sunny in Mexico City. The temperature is fifty-seven degrees Fahrenheit (fourteen degrees Celsius).
f) It's snowing in Toronto. The temperature is nineteen degrees Fahrenheit (minus seven degrees Celsius).
g) It's snowing in Montreal. The temperature is twelve degrees Fahrenheit (minus eleven degrees Celsius).
h) It's cloudy in New York (City). The temperature is twenty-eight degrees Fahrenheit (minus two degrees Celsius).
i) It's sunny in Miami. The temperature is sixty-six degrees Fahrenheit (nineteen degrees Celsius).
j) It's sunny in San Juan. The temperature is seventy degrees Fahrenheit (twenty-one degrees Celsius).

Unit 5
What are you doing?

1.
b) It's 11:00 A.M. in Denver. It's eleven o'clock in the morning.
c) It's 12:00 P.M. in Mexico City. It's noon.
d) It's 1:00 P.M. in Lima. It's one o'clock in the afternoon.
e) It's 2:00 P.M. in Santiago. It's two o'clock in the afternoon.
f) It's 3:00 P.M. in Rio de Janeiro. It's three o'clock in the afternoon.

2.
b) It's eleven thirty-five. / It's twenty-five to twelve.
c) It's four thirty.
d) It's eight forty-five. / It's a quarter to nine.
e) It's seven-oh-five. / It's five after seven.
f) It's nine fifty-five. / It's five to ten.

3.
b) He's wearing pajamas.
c) Tony is getting dressed.
d) She's reading the newspaper.
e) They're having breakfast.
f) Mrs. Peterson is carrying a briefcase.
g) She's wearing a suit.
h) She's going to work.
i) She's watching television / having a cup of coffee.
j) It's (time). I'm studying English / doing my homework. (Answers will vary.)

4.
b) It's four o'clock in the afternoon.
c) It's nine fifteen in the morning.
d) It's eight o'clock at night.
e) It's ten forty-five at night. *or* It's a quarter to eleven at night.
f) It's three thirty in the afternoon.

5.
b) Yes, he is.
c) No, it isn't. (*or* No, it's not.) It's raining.
d) No, they aren't. (*or* No, they're not.) They're watching television.
e) No, she isn't. (*or* No, she's not.) She's wearing shorts.
f) Yes, we are.

6.
b) Is Tai-lin wearing a raincoat?
   Yes, he is.
c) Is Rosa dancing?
   No, she isn't. She's talking on the telephone.
d) Are Terry and Helen eating?
   No, they aren't. They're dancing.
e) Are Pedro and Sonia talking?
   Yes, they are.
f) Is Brandon drinking?
   Yes, he is.
g) Is Carlos reading a (*or* the) newspaper?
   No, he isn't. He's reading a book.
h) Is Rosa wearing slacks?
   No, she isn't. She's wearing a dress.

Unit 6
How do you go to work?

1.
Maria: Do you live downtown, David?
David: Yes, I live with my mother. She <u>has</u> an apartment near here.
Maria: Oh, so you <u>walk</u> to work.
David: Actually, I <u>don't</u> walk to work in the morning. I <u>go</u> to work by <u>subway</u>, and then I <u>walk</u> home at night. What about you?
Maria: Well, my husband and I <u>have</u> a house in the suburbs now, so I <u>drive</u> my car to work.
David: Do you and your husband <u>drive</u> to work together?
Maria: No, he <u>doesn't</u> work downtown. He <u>works</u> in the suburbs near our house. And he <u>goes</u> to work by bus.

2.
b) Steve is Sam's brother.
c) Sam and Sharon are Amy's parents.
d) Kate is Amy's sister.
e) Barbara is Sharon's mother.

3.
Answers will vary.

4.
b) He goes to work at nine o'clock every day.
c) He has lunch at twelve o'clock (*or* at noon) every day.
d) He takes a break at three o'clock every day.
e) He leaves work at five o'clock every day.
f) He plays tennis at six o'clock on Mondays and Wednesdays.
g) He swims at six o'clock on Tuesdays and Thursdays.
h) He goes to a restaurant at six o'clock on Fridays.

5.
Answers will vary.

6.
b) Do you live with your parents?
c) Does your sister drive to work?
d) Do your parents watch television in the evening?
e) Does your mother have a job?
f) Does your mother use public transportation?
g) Does your father work on Saturdays?
h) Do you have a big dinner on Sundays?

7.
Answers will vary. Sample answers:
a) I get up at 7:00 A.M. every weekday.
b) I eat breakfast and read the newspaper every morning.
c) I go to the movies every Friday night.
d) I sleep late and listen to music every Sunday morning.

Unit 7
Does the apartment have a view?

1.
b) bedroom
c) porch
d) kitchen
e) dining room
f) living room
g) garage
h) basement
i) yard

2.
Mary: Do you live in the country, Jane?
Jane: No, I don't. I live in an apartment downtown.
Mary: Is it near here?
Jane: Yes, it is. It's next to the park.
Mary: Does your daughter live with you?
Jane: No, she doesn't. She has her own apartment now.
Mary: Oh, I see. Does your husband work downtown, too?
Jane: No, he doesn't. He's a writer, so he works at home. And he cleans the house every day.
Mary: Oh, you're lucky! I live alone and I clean my own house.

3.
b) Yes, I do. / No, I don't.
c) Yes, it does. / No, it doesn't.
d) Yes, it does. / No, it doesn't.
e) Yes, they do. / No, they don't.
f) Yes, I do. / No, I don't.
g) Yes, she/he does. / No, she/he doesn't.
h) Yes, we do. / No, we don't.
i) Yes, it does. / No, it doesn't.
j) Yes, it does. / No, it doesn't.

4.
In Roger's house, there's a big living room. There are two bedrooms and two bathrooms. There's no garden, but there's a balcony. There are lots of bookcases and books. There aren't any chairs in the kitchen, but there's a big table with chairs in the dining room. There's a microwave oven in the kitchen. There are two televisions in Roger's house – there's one television in the living room and one television in his bedroom.

5.
b) Yes, there's a dishwasher in my kitchen. /
No, there's no dishwasher in my kitchen.
c) Yes, there are armchairs in the living room. /
No, there aren't any armchairs in the living room.
d) Yes, there's a television in my living room. /
No, there's no television in my living room.
e) Yes, there's a mirror in the bathroom. /
No, there's no mirror in the bathroom.
f) Yes, there are pictures in my bedroom. /
No, there aren't any pictures in my bedroom.
g) Yes, there are closets in my bedroom. /
No, there aren't any closets in my bedroom.
h) Yes, there are bookcases in my bedroom. /
No, there aren't any bookcases in my bedroom.

6.
b) There aren't any chairs in the dining room.
c) There's a stove in the living room.
d) There's a refrigerator in the bedroom.
e) There's no bed in the bedroom.
f) There are armchairs in the bathroom.
Answers will vary for (g)–(j). Possible answers:
There's a bed in the kitchen.
There's a clock in the kitchen.
There's no refrigerator in the kitchen.
There's no table in the kitchen.
There's no stove in the kitchen.
There aren't any chairs in the kitchen.

Unit 8
What do you do?

1.

Across clues	*Down clues*
1 cashier	2 salesclerk
4 nurse	3 police officer
5 pilot	6 teacher
7 chef	
8 waiter	
9 singer	

2.
Sample answers:
b) He's a waiter.
   He works in a restaurant.
c) He's a singer.
   He sings (*or* works) in a nightclub.
d) She's a police officer.
   She wears a uniform.
e) She's a chef.
   She works in a restaurant.
   She wears a hat.
f) They're pilots.
   They wear uniforms.

3.
b) What do Kelly and Pam do?
Where do they work?
c) Where does your son work?
What does he do there?
d) Where do you work?
What do you do there?

4.
b) safe
c) boring
d) pleasant
e) difficult
f) relaxing

5.
Answers will vary. Sample answers:
b) A lawyer has a high salary.
c) A teacher's salary is low.
d) Stephanie has nice students.
e) Linda's apartment is small.
f) Chris has a big house.
g) Charles has a gray car.
h) Sarah's friend is Japanese.

6.
Sample answers:
b) I live in a big apartment.
c) I live in a pleasant town.
d) I have a Japanese friend, two French friends, and three Chilean friends.

Unit 9
I love strawberries!

1.
b) butter
c) cheese
d) milk
e) broccoli
f) tomato
g) carrot
h) bread
i) pasta
j) rice
k) apple
l) orange
m) banana
n) beef
o) fish
p) egg
q) chicken

2.
Answers will vary.

3.
Answers will vary, but all answers begin as follows:
a) I think oranges are . . .
b) I think cheese is . . .
c) I think hamburgers are . . .
d) I think broccoli is . . .
e) I think fish is . . .
f) I think chocolate is . . .
g) I think Chinese food is . . .
h) I think Mexican food is . . .
i) I think Italian food is . . .

4.
b) bananas
c) carrots
d) strawberries
e) tomatoes
f) pasta
g) potatoes
h) mangoes

5.
I usually eat a healthy breakfast. I always have some fruit. I usually have an apple or a banana. I also have some bread, but I don't have any butter on my bread. And I don't have any meat or eggs. I have some juice and coffee, but I don't have any milk in my coffee. I sometimes have a cookie. I know it's not good for me, but it's delicious!

6.
b) In China, people seldom put milk in tea.
c) In England, people usually put milk in tea.
d) In Japan, people sometimes have fish for breakfast.
e) In Korea, people often eat pickled vegetables.
f) In Brazil, people often make drinks with fruit.
g) People don't usually have ice cream for breakfast.
h) Vegetarians never eat meat.

7.
Answers will vary.

8.
Sample answers:
b) *a sandwich*
You need some bread.
You need some meat or some cheese.
You don't need any chocolate.
c) *vegetable soup*
You need some onions, some carrots, and some tomatoes.
You need some water.
You don't need any fruit.
d) *a green salad*
You need some lettuce.
You need some oil and vinegar.
You don't need any bananas.
e) Answers will vary.

Unit 10
Can you swim very well?

1.
b) Can Simon and Victor swim?
   Yes, they can.
c) Can Andrew play the piano?
   Yes, he can.
d) Can Alicia cook?
   No, she can't.
e) Can Sue and Lisa draw?
   No, they can't.
f) Can Alan ice-skate?
   Yes, he can.

2.
b) Judy can draw. Tim can draw, too.
c) Judy can cook. Tim can cook, too.
d) Tim can't ice-skate. Judy can't ice-skate, either.

3.
b) Yes, I can. / No, I can't.
c) Yes, I can. / No, I can't.
d) Yes, I am. / No, I'm not.
e) Yes, I am. / No, I'm not.
f) Yes, I can. / No, I can't.
g) Yes, I do. / No, I don't.
h) Yes, I can. / No, I can't.

4.
b) Laura and Mark are running (*or* jogging).
c) Amy and Matthew are playing volleyball.
d) Daniel is swimming.
e) Katherine is drawing a picture (*or* writing a letter).
f) Chris is playing cards.
g) Keiko and Kenji are reading.
h) Susan and Peter are playing chess.

5.
Answers to the questions will vary.
b) Are you good at basketball?
c) Can you play the piano?
d) Do you know how to cook French food?
e) What do you know how to cook?
f) Are you good at math?

6.
Answers will vary. Sample answers:
b) I'm good at team sports. I can play baseball and basketball.
c) I'm not good at individual sports. I don't know how to play golf or tennis.
d) I'm good at winter sports. I can ski and ice-skate.
e) I'm not good at board games. I don't know how to play chess.
f) I'm good at languages. I can speak French and Russian. I'm learning English.

Unit 11
When's your birthday?

1.
a) January
b) February
c) March
d) April
e) May
f) June
g) July
h) August
i) September
j) October
k) November
l) December

2.
b) September eleventh
c) January sixteenth
d) February ninth
e) October twelfth
f) May tenth
g) July twentieth
h) August twenty-third

3.
b) Anita is going to be twenty-six on July twenty-seventh.
c) Toshi is going to be fifty-one on May fifteenth.
d) Peggy is going to be nineteen on September thirteenth.
e) Miguel is going to be twenty-one on April first.
f) Mei is going to be forty-six on August twenty-second.

4.
Answers will vary. Sample answers:
b) I'm going to have a party on my best friend's birthday.
c) I'm going to stay at home tonight.
d) I'm going to see a movie tomorrow.
e) I'm going to go to the park next Saturday.
f) I'm going to go out with friends next Sunday.
g) I'm going to go to the beach next summer.
h) I'm going to stay up all night on New Year's Eve.

5.
b) On March fourth, she's going to have lunch with Tony at noon.
c) On March fifth, she's going to have a meeting.
d) On March sixth, she's going to see a movie with Kate in the evening.
e) On March seventh, she's going to take a computer course.
f) On March eighth, she's going to go to Sam's party in the evening.
g) On March ninth, she's going to have a picnic with Tony and Sonia.

6.

Answers will vary. Sample answers:

b) I'm going to go to the pool. I'm going to go swimming.
c) I'm going to go to the park. I'm going to have a picnic.
d) I'm going to sleep in.
e) I'm going to have a snack. I'm going to watch television.
f) I'm going to go to the store. I'm going to buy some food.
g) We're going to play tennis. We're going to go to the beach.
h) I'm going to read a book. I'm going to relax.

7.

a)

Sandra: What are you going to do this weekend, Eric?
Eric: I'm going to go to the country with my brother.
Sandra: That's nice. Where are you going to stay?
Eric: We're going to stay at my aunt's house. She lives in the country.
Sandra: Really? What are you going to do?
Eric: I think we're going to go mountain climbing.
Sandra: Is your aunt going to go with you?
Eric: No, my aunt isn't going to come with us. She can't. She's eighty-two years old!

b)

Scott: I'm going to have a birthday party for Kathleen next Saturday.
Patricia: Oh! How old is she going to be?
Scott: She's going to be twenty-one. Can you come?
Patricia: Sure! Where is it going to be?
Scott: It's going to be at my house. Do you have the address?
Patricia: Yes, I do. And what time is it going to start?
Scott: It's going to start at seven o'clock.
Patricia: Is Bob going to come?
Scott: No, Bob is going to work on Saturday, so he can't come.
Patricia: That's too bad. Well, thanks for the invitation. See you on Saturday.

Unit 12
What's the matter?

1.

b) eye
c) mouth
d) neck
e) arm
f) stomach
g) leg
h) foot
i) feet
j) hand
k) shoulder
l) teeth
m) nose
n) ear
o) hair

2.

b) Drink some hot tea. I hope you feel better soon.
c) Listen. Come to my house and we can talk.
d) That's too bad. Maybe the teacher can help you.
e) I'm happy to hear that.
f) I hope you sleep better tonight.

3.

I live in the suburbs. On weekdays, I get up at 7 A.M. I take the train to the city at 8:15. I leave my office at five o'clock in the afternoon, except on Fridays, when I leave at three. I usually go to bed at 10:30 P.M., but in the summer I often go to bed late. On Saturdays I stay home, but on Sundays I play golf with my friend Bob. We're going to play in a big tournament on July 15th this year. We have to get up early – it starts at seven o'clock in the morning!

4.

Answers will vary. Sample answers:

b) I have English class on (Mondays and Wednesdays).
c) My birthday is on (September 1st).
d) I usually go to bed at (eleven o'clock).
e) My favorite television show is on (Wednesday) at (9:00 P.M.).
f) I usually take my vacation in (the summer/August).
g) This class ends in (June).

5.

Receptionist: Hello, can I help you?
Rose: Yes, can I see the doctor today, please?
Receptionist: Yes, how about this afternoon at 2:30?
Rose: That's fine.
Receptionist: Can I have your name, please?
Rose: My name's Rose Foster.
Receptionist: All right, Ms. Foster. Thank you.
Rose: Thank you. Good-bye.

6.
Sample answers:
a) Make a shopping list.
Go to the store.
Buy some meat and vegetables.
b) Stay home and rest.
Don't go to work.
Drink some hot tea.
c) Get some exercise every day.
Have a good breakfast.
Eat lots of vegetables.
d) Take a hot bath and relax.
Telephone a friend.
Go to the movies with some friends.

Unit 13
Can you help me, please?

1.

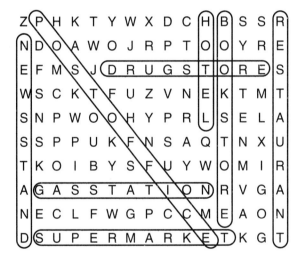

b) You can stay at a hotel on your vacation.
c) You can buy a newspaper at a newsstand.
d) You can have dinner at a restaurant.
e) You can buy stamps at a post office.
f) You can buy gasoline at a gas station.
g) You can buy a book at a bookstore.
h) You can buy potatoes at a supermarket.

2.
b) bookstore
c) post office
d) drugstore
e) supermarket
f) hotel
g) gas station
h) newsstand

3.
Answers will vary. Sample answers:
b) There's a supermarket on the corner of Diane Street and Fourth Avenue. It's next to the cafe.
c) There's a department store on Beatrice Street / on the corner of Beatrice Street and Fifth Avenue. It's next to the drugstore.
d) There's a gas station on the corner of Ann Street and Fourth Avenue. It's behind the Mexican restaurant.
e) There's a Mexican restaurant on the corner of Beatrice Street and Fourth Avenue. It's next to the drugstore / in front of the gas station.
f) There's a hotel on Catherine Street. It's across from the park.
g) There's a post office on Diane Street. It's next to the coffee shop.
h) There's a drugstore on Beatrice Street. It's between the Mexican restaurant and the department store.

4.
Answers will vary. Sample answers:
b) Walk down Sixth Avenue to Diane Street. Turn left. Walk for one block. It's on the left.
c) Walk for one block to Sixth Avenue. Turn left. Walk for one block. The park is on the right, on the corner of Sixth Avenue and Catherine Street.
d) Walk down Fifth Avenue to Diane Street. Turn right. Walk for one block. It's on the right.
e) Turn right on Catherine Street. Walk for two blocks. Turn left. Walk up Sixth Avenue to Barbara Street. Turn right. It's on the left.

5.
Sample answers:
a)
Man: Excuse me. Is there a supermarket near here?
Woman: Yes, there's a supermarket on the corner of Diane Street and Fourth Avenue.
Man: Thank you. And is there a bookstore near the supermarket?
Woman: Yes, there's a bookstore on the corner of Catherine Street and Fifth Avenue.
b)
Man: Is there a good Mexican restaurant near here?
Woman: Yes, there's a good Mexican restaurant on the corner of Beatrice Street and Fourth Avenue.
Man: Thank you. And is there a drugstore near the restaurant?
Woman: Yes, there's a drugstore next to the restaurant, on Beatrice Street.
c)
1st Woman: Excuse me. Is there a hotel near here?
2nd Woman: Yes, there's a hotel on Catherine Street.
1st Woman: And is there a park near the hotel?
2nd Woman: Yes, there's a park across from the hotel.
1st Woman: Thank you.

Unit 14
Did you have a good weekend?

1.

/t/	/d/	/ɪd/
asked	cleaned	hated
cooked	exercised	invited
fixed	listened	started
walked	played	visited
watched	stayed	
worked	studied	

2.
a) stayed, watched
b) played, asked
c) started, worked, exercised
d) cleaned, visited
e) hated
f) walked, listened

3.
b) Carol cleaned (her kitchen) last weekend. Max didn't clean last weekend.
c) Carol didn't play golf last weekend. Max played golf (last weekend).
d) Carol cooked last weekend. Max cooked, too.
e) Carol listened to music last weekend. Max didn't listen to music last weekend.
f) Carol didn't walk in the park last weekend. Max walked in the park last weekend.
g) Carol didn't watch television last weekend. Max watched television last weekend.

4.

Present tense	Past tense	Present tense	Past tense
drink	drank	see	saw
drive	drove	sleep	slept
eat	ate	take	took
get	got	teach	taught
have	had	tell	told
know	knew	think	thought
put	put	wear	wore
say	said	write	wrote

5.
b) Did you sleep well last night?
Yes, I did. / No, I didn't.
c) Did you get any exercise yesterday?
Yes, I did. / No, I didn't.
d) Did you eat any vegetables yesterday?
Yes, I did. / No, I didn't.
e) Did you have a good breakfast this morning?
Yes, I did. / No, I didn't.
f) Did you drink any juice this morning?
Yes, I did. / No, I didn't.

6.
b) On Saturday morning, she exercised.
c) On Saturday afternoon, she wrote a letter.
d) On Saturday night, she went to a Chinese restaurant (with a friend).
e) On Sunday morning, she got up at 11:30.
f) On Sunday afternoon, she read the newspaper.
g) On Sunday afternoon, she took a nap / she slept.
h) On Sunday night, she went to the movies.

7.
Answers will vary.

Unit 15
Where were you born?

1.
a)
Peter: Were you at home on the weekend?
David: No, I wasn't. I was in the country.
Peter: Really? Were you with your family?
David: Yes, I was. I was with my sister and her family.
b)
Sue: Were your parents born in the U.S.?
Kim: No, they weren't. They were born in China.
Sue: Really? And were you born in China, too?
Kim: No, I wasn't. I was born in New York.
c)
Nancy: Were you in college last year?
Chuck: No, I wasn't. I graduated two years ago.
Nancy: So where were you last year?
Chuck: I was in Europe. I had a job in a hotel.
d)
Bob: Were you good at sports in high school?
Jim: Yes, I was. I played football.
Bob: And were your brothers good at sports, too?
Jim: No, they weren't. They never liked sports in high school.

2.
b) nineteen eighty-five
c) seventeen fifty-three
d) fourteen twenty-seven
f) 1840
g) 1962
h) 1710

3.

b) Audrey Hepburn was an actress. She was born in 1929 in Belgium. She was in the movie *Breakfast at Tiffany's* in 1961.

c) Arthur Ashe was a tennis player. He was born in 1943 in the United States. He won the Wimbledon tennis championship in 1975.

d) Frida Kahlo was an artist. She was born in 1907 in Mexico. She painted *Diego and I* in 1949.

e) Marie Curie was a scientist. She was born in 1867 in Poland. She won the Nobel Prize for Chemistry in 1911.

f) Ernest Hemingway was a novelist. He was born in 1899 in the United States. He wrote the novel *The Old Man and the Sea* in 1952.

4.

A: Where did you go to high school?
B: In California.
A: What was your favorite sport in high school?
B: It was tennis.
A: Who was your favorite teacher in high school?
B: My math teacher, Mrs. Duran.
A: When did you graduate from high school?
B: In 1985.
A: How old were you when you graduated?
B: I was eighteen years old.
A: What did you study in college?
B: I studied engineering.
A: Why did you study engineering?
B: Because I was good at math.
A: How were your professors in college?
B: They were excellent.

5.

Answers to the questions will vary.

b) Where were you at midnight last night / last night at midnight? I was . . .

c) How was your weekend? It was . . .

d) What did you do on the weekend? I . . .

e) How old were you on your last birthday? I was . . .

f) When was your last vacation? It was . . .

g) Where did you go on your vacation? I . . .

6.

A: How was your vacation?
B: My vacation was great, thanks!
A: Where did you go?
B: I went to Canada.
A: How did you get there?
B: I went by plane.
A: Where did you stay?
B: I stayed at a small hotel in Vancouver.
A: How was the weather?
B: The weather was good, but it rained for two days.
A: Why did you go to Vancouver?
B: I went to Vancouver because I have some friends there.
A: When did you come home?
B: I came home yesterday. It's nice to be home.

7.

Helen Keller was born in 1880 in the United States. Her father was a captain in the army and her parents were quite rich. Helen became blind and deaf when she was nineteen months old. A woman called Annie Sullivan was her teacher. Annie Sullivan taught Helen Keller how to speak. Helen Keller graduated from Radcliffe College in 1904. She wrote a book called *The Story of My Life* in 1902. During her life, she visited many countries and spoke about being blind and deaf.

Unit 16
Hello. Is Jennifer there, please?

1.

Claire: Hello. Is Linda there, please?
Bill: I'm sorry. Linda's not here right now.
Claire: Oh. Can I leave her a message?
Bill: Sure. What's the message?
Claire: Please ask her to call Claire. My number is 555-7092.
Bill: 555-7092. OK.
Claire: Thank you very much.
Bill: You're welcome. Good-bye.

2.

a)

Hi, Jim. This is Bob. My friend Alex is visiting me, and we're going to see a movie tomorrow. Do you want to see it with us? The movie is called *Lucky Stars*, and it's a comedy. Please call us today, if possible. I hope you can come.

b)

Hi, Bob. Thanks for the message. I'm sorry, but I can't go to the movie with you. Susan is in town and I'm going to go out with her. We have to talk to her parents, so we're going to have dinner with them. Guess what! I asked her to marry me, and she said yes. But say hello to Alex for me. I remember him well. He's a lot of fun.

3.
b)
Scott: Hello, Diana, this is Scott. Is Carmen there?
Diana: Hi, Scott. No, she's not. She and Elena <u>are at the mall.</u>
c)
Scott: Hi, Mrs. Avona. This is Scott Gilbert. Is Donna there, please?
Mrs. A.: I'm sorry, Scott, she's not here. She<u>'s in the hospital.</u>
d)
Scott: Hello, Mrs. Sharpe. Is Sandy there, please?
Mrs. S.: No, I'm sorry, she isn't. She<u>'s in class.</u>
e)
Scott: Hello, Mr. Carson. <u>Is Jeff there, please?</u>
Mr. C.: I'm sorry. Jeff isn't here. He<u>'s at work.</u>
f)
Scott: Hello, Mrs. Wen. This is <u>Scott Gilbert. Is John there, please?</u>
Mrs. W.: I'm sorry, Scott. John <u>is on vacation.</u>

4.
Answers will vary.

5.
Answers will vary.

6.

Across clues		*Down clues*	
3	know	1	chairs
5	sixth	2	bought
6	uniform	4	weren't
7	talking	5	sat
8	drink	8	degrees
11	Central	9	wearing
13	message	10	drugstore
14	neighbor	12	bananas
16	stressful	15	his